Step by Step

Home Networking

with Microsoft® Windows® XP

**Matthew Danda and
Heather T. Brown**

PUBLISHED BY
Microsoft Press
A Division of Microsoft Corporation
One Microsoft Way
Redmond, Washington 98052-6399

Library of Congress Cataloging-in-Publication Data
Danda, Matthew, 1971-
    Home Networking with Microsoft Windows XP Step by Step / Matthew Danda, Heather
  T. Brown.
        p. cm.
    Includes index.
    ISBN 0-7356-1435-0
    1. Home computer networks.   2. Microsoft Windows XP.   I. Brown, Heather T., 1971-
II. Title.

TK5105.75 .D35   2001
004.6'8--dc21   2001044367

Printed and bound in the United States of America.

1 2 3 4 5 6 7 8 9   QWT   6 5 4 3 2

Distributed in Canada by Penguin Books Canada Limited.

A CIP catalogue record for this book is available from the British Library.

Microsoft Press books are available through booksellers and distributors worldwide. For further informa-
tion about international editions, contact your local Microsoft Corporation office or contact Microsoft
Press International directly at fax (425) 706-7329. Visit our Web site at www.microsoft.com/mspress.
Send comments to *mspinput@microsoft.com*.

DirectX, Hotmail, Microsoft, Microsoft Press, MS-DOS, MSN, Outlook, PowerPoint, Windows, and
Windows Media are either registered trademarks or trademarks of Microsoft Corporation in the United
States and/or other countries. Other product and company names mentioned herein may be the trademarks
of their respective owners.

The example companies, organizations, products, domain names, e-mail addresses, logos, people, places,
and events depicted herein are fictitious. No association with any real company, organization, product,
domain name, e-mail address, logo, person, place, or event is intended or should be inferred.

Acquisitions Editor: Alex Blanton
Project Editor: Jenny Moss Benson
Interior design and illustration: James D. Kramer

Body Part No. X08-50940

Contents

What's New with Networking in Microsoft Windows XP

Microsoft Windows XP has a new look! Not only has Windows XP cleaned up your desktop, but now operating system tasks that you perform frequently are easier to find. In all the folders, look for the most commonly used tasks in the Tasks list located in the left pane. And what's included with Windows XP for home networking is even better. Easier wizards, new security features, and some new advanced networking features make this a great time to start networking computers in your home.

Tip

To use this book, you will need at least one computer that uses Windows XP Home Edition or Professional, and at least one other computer with Microsoft Windows 98, Microsoft Windows 98 Second Edition, Microsoft Windows Millennium Edition (Me), or Windows XP on it. The exercises throughout this book use Windows XP Home Edition and Windows 98 Second Edition to demonstrate how to create your home network. The procedures you use to network other Windows operating systems with Windows XP are either the same or very similar.

So, what's new with home networking in Windows XP? First, you can take advantage of improved Plug and Play technology. When you plug in your network hardware, Windows XP finds it, installs it, and tells you if it needs any disks. Most network hardware is installed without any interaction from you. Once your network hardware is installed, Windows XP can detect if it's plugged in. If you have problems with your network, you can easily confirm that your network hardware is installed, plugged in, and correctly configured.

The simplified Network Setup Wizard is smarter than ever. With a few clicks of your mouse, the Network Setup Wizard helps you choose the right options, set up Internet Connection Sharing, share your files and printers, and make your network secure. In addition, you can use your Windows XP CD to add computers with other supported Windows operating systems to your network, or you can create a floppy Network Setup Disk. The Network Setup Wizard walks you through network setup on each computer that you want to add to your network.

Once your network is set up, advanced networking features in Windows XP let you create a network bridge, easily set up a wireless network, and make Internet gaming a seamless and secure experience. Plus, you can use the new Internet features of Windows XP—such as Windows Messenger's voice and video capabilities—from all the computers on your home network.

As you start using your network, you will find that you can quickly access shared files on all the computers on the network. The Network Setup Wizard creates a single Shared Documents folder on each computer from which you can share files with the other computers on your network. Just drop the files into the Shared Documents folder, and you are ready to go.

Another new feature in Windows XP is automatic discovery of printers. When you add a printer to a computer that is on your network, the printer is automatically made available to the other computers on the network.

How to Use This Book

This *Step by Step* book walks you through setting up and using a home network. To use this book, you should work through the first five chapters in order. Start with Chapter 1, "Introduction to Home Networking," for an introduction to home networking. Then get busy with Chapter 2, "Connecting Your Computers Together." (You may need to make a trip to the computer store to buy some computer hardware.) Chapter 3, "Connecting to the Internet," helps you get connected to the Internet. Chapter 4, "Installing the Home Networking Software," and Chapter 5, "Securing Your Home Network," help you get all your computers and peripherals working together and then make them secure.

After your network is set up, you can skip around Chapters 6, 7, and 8 to start understanding how to use your network. Chapter 6, "Sharing Data on the Network," and Chapter 7, "Sharing Printers and Other Peripherals," help you get the most out of your home network by showing you how to share files, printers, and other peripherals. Chapter 8, "Communicating and Collaborating with Others on Your Network," extends your networking experience to the Internet, where you can take advantage of some great features that are provided by the Microsoft Network (MSN), such as Windows Messenger.

Getting Help

Every effort has been made to ensure the accuracy of this book. If you do run into problems, please contact the appropriate source for help and assistance.

Getting Help with This Book

If your question or issue concerns the content of this book, please first search the online Microsoft Knowledge Base, which provides support information for known errors in or corrections to this book, at the following Web site:

http://www.microsoft.com/mspress/support/search.asp

If you do not find your answer at the online Knowledge Base, send your comments or questions to Microsoft Press Technical Support at:

mspinput@microsoft.com

Getting Help with Microsoft Windows XP

If your question is about a Microsoft product, including Microsoft Windows XP, and not about the content of this Microsoft Press book, please search the Microsoft Knowledge Base at:

http://support.microsoft.com/directory

In the United States, Microsoft software product support issues not covered by the Microsoft Knowledge Base are addressed by Microsoft Product Support Services. The Microsoft software support options available from Microsoft Product Support Services are listed at:

http://support.microsoft.com/directory

Outside the United States, for support information specific to your location, please refer to the Worldwide Support menu on the Microsoft Product Support Services Web site for the site specific to your country:

http://support.microsoft.com/directory

Conventions and Features

You can save time when you use this book by understanding how the *Step by Step* series shows special instructions, keys to press, buttons to click, and so on.

Convention	Meaning
1 **2**	Numbered steps guide you through hands-on exercises in each topic.
●	A round bullet indicates an exercise that has only one step.
Tip	This section provides a helpful hint or shortcut that makes working through a task easier
Important	This section points out information that you need to know to complete the procedure.
Troubleshooting	This section shows you how to fix a common problem.
Close ⊠	When a button is referenced in a topic, a picture of the button appears in the margin.
Alt+Tab	A plus sign (+) between two key names means that you must press those keys at the same time. For example, "Press Alt+Tab" means that you hold down the Alt key while you press Tab.
Boldface type	Terms explained in the glossary are shown in blue boldface type.
Italic type	URLs, emphasized words, and text you are supposed to type appear in italic type.

Chapter 1
Introduction to Home Networking

Are you making the most of your home computers? By creating a home network, you can make your computers more convenient, cost effective, and fun to use. With a Microsoft Windows XP computer as part of your network, setting up a home network is easier than ever. Even if you have a wide variety of new and old computers with different operating systems, Windows XP makes it easy to quickly start taking advantage of the benefits of home networking.

In this chapter, you'll learn the advantages of creating a home network with Windows XP.

The Emergence of Home Networks

In the past, a typical family might have felt lucky to have just one computer in the home. Today, as computers extend further into our everyday lives, more and more families are acquiring multiple computers. For example, you and your spouse might have laptops that you bring home from work, the family might have a desktop computer for **Internet surfing** and balancing the checkbook, and your children might have a computer for schoolwork and playing games. However, having multiple computers doesn't necessarily mean that you're making the most of the new home networking technologies.

A computer by itself is only as powerful as its hardware and the software and information it contains. But if you connect two or more computers together to form a network, each computer becomes more powerful because it can share information and resources with the others. For example, with computers on a network, you can exchange files with a few clicks of the mouse, instead of having to use floppy disks to transfer information from computer to computer.

Important

You might not be able to share some programs across a network, due to product licensing requirements. Before using a particular program on more than one of your computers, be sure to check the product licensing agreement. This agreement, sometimes called the End User License Agreement, typically appears on your screen during the installation process. A copy of it might also be included with the printed documentation that accompanied the product when you bought it.

Files aren't the only thing you can share. You can use a printer or disk drive attached to another computer on the network just as easily as if it were connected to your computer. Or you can share a single Internet connection with all the computers in the home. Because computers on a network can share information and **peripherals**, such as modems, recordable CD drives, and printers, you don't need to spend money purchasing more than one of each type of hardware device for your home. This makes using a home network both convenient and cost effective.

Advantages of Home Networking

By creating a home network, you allow each of your computers to share information and hardware devices with the other computers. You also create exciting new ways to communicate and interact with people. Some of the advantages of home networking include:

- *Sharing an Internet connection* All the computers on the network can share a single **Internet connection**. This means that you need to set up only one Internet connection for the entire network, instead of setting up an Internet connection on every computer and then fighting for the phone line.

- *Sharing files and folders* You can view, modify, and copy files stored on a different computer on the network just as easily as if they were stored on your computer.

- *Sharing printers* There is no need to purchase a second color printer or laser printer if you already own one. You can print on any printer connected to any computer on a network just as easily as printing on a printer connected directly to your computer.

- *Communicating with others* Using programs that come with Windows XP, you can keep in touch with friends and family through the network and through the Internet. You can use **Microsoft Outlook Express** to send and receive e-mail messages on the Internet, and you can converse and exchange information with others in real time using **Microsoft Windows Messenger**.

The Future of Networking in Your Home

When networking in the home first began, the focus was on sharing information between computers. Just being able to transfer files between computers was a major advantage. Before long, it became clear that sharing devices such as printers, removable storage devices, and other computer peripherals added even more value to a home network.

At the same time home computer networking was coming of age, the idea of being able to control the home with a computer was being adopted by computer junkies and other people who were into the nitty-gritty of how computers work. The thought of turning lights on and off and monitoring security cameras with a computer was a hobbyist's dream. Until recently, the concept of home control hasn't been taken into the mainstream, but now home control is being introduced to the less technical consumer. Small devices such as light switches and security cameras are becoming easier to add to your home network.

The home networking industry is now gearing up for the next evolution in home networking technology. In the future, you will see home networking capabilities in many home appliances and other consumer devices not normally associated with computers. For example, your washing machine, television, or even your garage door opener will be able to talk to your computer and then communicate with you! Ever wonder if your garage door is open as you drive down the freeway? Ever start your washing machine, only to find out two hours later that you forgot to close the lid? With advances in home control, these annoyances will be a thing of the past. Your appliances and electronic devices will be able to communicate with the network, and then relay that information to you. In addition, as computers reach their potential as a means of communication, expect to see traditional means of communication—the telephone and television—continue to be supplanted by Internet chat programs and interactive multimedia Web sites.

To enable these scenarios in the home, over 350 companies have come together to form the **Universal Plug and Play (UPnP) Forum** (*www.upnp.org*). The UPnP forum is developing a standard for the home networking industry that will make it a snap to add intelligent home devices to your home network. In the future, you will be able to bring home a new UPnP-enabled DVD player, plug it in, and have any UPnP-enabled televisions and computers on your home network recognize that it's available and use it. You will then be able to watch a DVD anywhere in your home with ease. Or maybe you will be on vacation and will wonder if your house sitter is really watering the plants. Not a problem; plug in your UPnP-enabled cameras, and you will be able to see what's going on at home by viewing the cameras on your home network from any Web browser.

■ *Network games* Computer games have been around as long as home computers themselves. However, the recent popularity of networks and the Internet has ushered in a new form of computer entertainment: the multi-player network game. Some of these games allow you to play with others on a network, while others allow you to play with larger groups of people on the Internet.

■ *Home automation* Believe it or not, you can connect other devices besides computers to your network and control them using your computer. For example, you can purchase devices that allow you to use your computer to control lights and appliances in your home. As more products emerge that take advantage of this new technology, expect to see new and exciting ways to use computers to automate your home.

Home Networking with Windows XP

Computer networks have been around for many years. In the past, only the most technical of computer users dared to create a computer network. However, as the number of uses for home computer networks increases, the demand for simple ways to create networks also increases. To meet this demand, Windows XP offers significant improvements in its networking features over previous versions of Windows.

It doesn't matter what types of Windows computers you already own. All you need is at least one Windows XP computer and the appropriate network hardware, and you can connect your computers together with a minimum of fuss. Adding additional Microsoft Windows 98, Microsoft Windows Millennium Edition (Me), and Microsoft Windows XP computers to your network is especially easy. The Windows XP Network Setup Wizard takes you through all the steps of setting up your home network, simplifying the tasks of home network setup, adding new computers to the network, and even taking advantage of advanced networking features.

A home network with at least one Windows XP computer can support all the advantages of home networking mentioned in the previous section. In addition, Windows XP offers a built-in firewall to help protect your network against hackers who might try to gain access via your Internet connection. Windows XP also provides a built-in **network bridge**, which allows you to use different types of network hardware on the same network. By supporting **Plug and Play** features, Windows XP makes it easy to set up your network hardware.

Home networking is just starting to realize its full potential. Start taking advantage of this new technology now, and watch how easy it is to make your home into the smart home of the future.

To create a home network using Windows XP, you need to follow this process:

1   Decide which type of network to use (described in Chapter 2, "Connecting Your Computers Together").

2   Purchase the appropriate network hardware, and install it on each computer that you want to connect to the network (also described in Chapter 2).

3   To use your Windows XP computer as the Internet connection host for the network, connect that computer to the Internet (described in Chapter 3, "Connecting to the Internet").

4   Run the Network Setup Wizard on the Windows XP computer (described in Chapter 4, "Installing the Home Networking Software").

5   Run the Network Setup Wizard on each computer that you want to connect to the network (also described in Chapter 4).

6   Configure and use the network, including sharing files and folders, sharing printers and other peripherals, and using the network to communicate with others (described in Chapters 5 through 8).

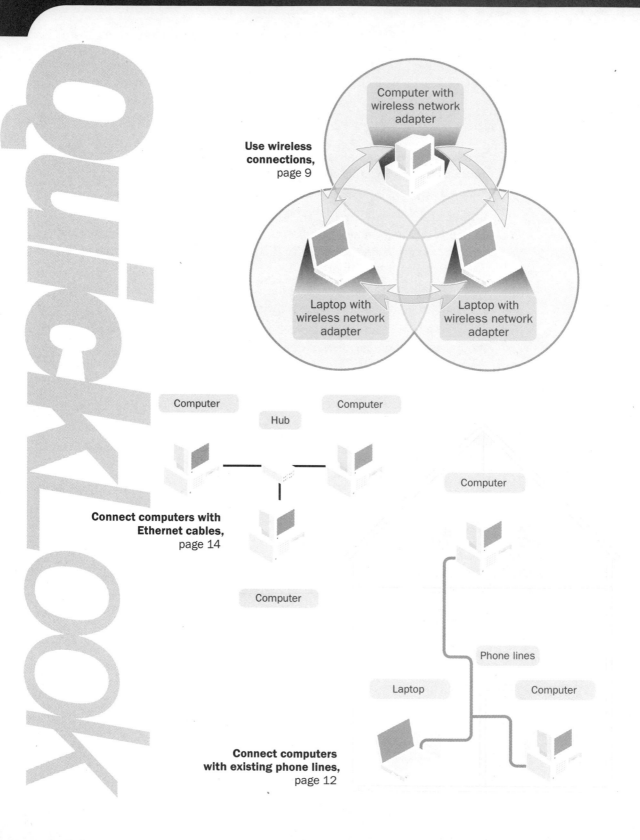

QuickLook

Use wireless connections, page 9

Computer with wireless network adapter

Laptop with wireless network adapter

Laptop with wireless network adapter

Computer

Hub

Computer

Connect computers with Ethernet cables, page 14

Computer

Computer

Phone lines

Laptop

Computer

Connect computers with existing phone lines, page 12

Chapter 2
Connecting Your Computers Together

After completing this chapter, you will be able to:

✔   **Choose a type of network to use: wireless, phoneline, or Ethernet**

✔   **Install a network adapter**

✔   **Connect two computers together directly**

✔   **Understand the importance of Internet security**

You've taken the leap and are ready to get started with the Microsoft Windows XP operating system. Now you're wondering how to connect your Windows XP computer to all the other computers in your home. Before you can take advantage of the new networking features, you need to physically connect your computers together with the necessary networking hardware. Sound like a daunting task? Don't worry; Windows XP provides powerful tools that make the process easy.

In this chapter, you'll learn how to make the connections, including how to choose the best type of network and how to install a network adapter. In addition, if you're looking for a quick solution, you'll learn how to connect two computers together without creating a network.

Tip

Many companies sell home networking kits that include all the hardware you need to connect two computers. Some kits also include additional software to help you set up and use a network. While these kits can be a good value, keep in mind that you do not need to purchase a kit that includes its own software, because Windows XP provides all the networking software you need.

Choosing a Type of Network

The first step in creating a home network is to decide what type of network to use, and the second is to install the necessary network hardware. Once you've completed these two tasks, you can set up the Windows XP network software and begin to use your network.

If you've ever walked down the networking aisle of your favorite computer store, you have probably seen a wide variety of network adapters, **network media** (such as cables), and network kits. It can get confusing trying to sort them all out. To help you choose among the different types of networks, take a moment to consider the following questions:

■ What are you using your network for? If you are using it to share an Internet connection, your network needs to be only as fast as your Internet connection. If you are going to transfer large files, such as video or pictures, faster network speeds will greatly improve your experience. (Network speed is measured in megabits per second, or **Mbps**.)

■ Are you comfortable running a lot of new cables through your home?

■ How much are you willing to spend?

To answer these questions and make your decision, take a moment to create an inventory of all of your current hardware, and consider where each computer will be located in the home. Keep in mind where power outlets and phone lines are located, and consider the feasibility of running cables between computers in your home. After you have all these factors in mind, you can decide which type of network is best for you.

Currently, three main types of networks are suitable for home use: wireless, phone-line, and Ethernet. Each uses a different type of hardware to connect the computers, and each can vary widely in cost, setup effort, and communication speed.

Tip

The computers on your home network can use a combination of different types of network connections. For more information, see "Using Multiple Types of Networks," later in this chapter.

The following sections in this chapter describe the characteristics of each type of connection in more detail. You can use the table on the facing page to quickly see the different types of networks and some advantages and disadvantages of each.

Name	Relative Cost	Speed	Advantages	Disadvantages
Wireless	Medium/High	Medium (11 Mbps)	Very easy to set up; does not require cables	Slower than Fast Ethernet and typically the most expensive type of connection
Phoneline	Low	Medium (up to 10 Mbps)	Easy to set up if phone lines are conveniently located	Slower than Fast Ethernet; might require installation of new phone lines in the home
Ethernet/ Fast Ethernet	Low/Medium	Medium/Fast (10 Mbps for Ethernet, 100 Mbps for Fast Ethernet)	Industry standard technology that's reliable and easy to set up	Requires running a cable from a central hub to each computer on the network, which might require installation of new cables in the home

Tip

Another type of network connection uses the power lines in your home. So far this type of network is quite slow and is not widely available; however, new versions of this technology promise improvements.

Using a Wireless Network

In terms of convenience, a wireless network is the easiest type to install in your home. A computer on a wireless network uses a special network adapter that sends radio waves through the air. Any other computer within range that also has a wireless network adapter can receive the transmissions and communicate successfully, even if the computers are separated by floors, ceilings, and walls. Although this system is the easiest to implement—because you don't need to worry about cables—it also tends to be the most expensive option, and it is limited by the distance between computers.

Various companies and industry groups have come together to create standards for wireless networking. The standard that's emerging as the leader is 802.11b, or WiFi, which offers speeds of up to 11 Mbps. (This technology was developed by the same organization that developed Ethernet, the **Institute of Electrical and Electronics Engineers, Inc. (IEEE)**. The name *WiFi* is short for "Wireless Ethernet.")

Types of WiFi Networks: Ad Hoc and Infrastructure

You can choose between two different types of WiFi networks: ad hoc and infrastructure. In an ad hoc network, every computer with a wireless network adapter communicates directly with every other computer with a wireless adapter. For this system to work, each computer must be within range of the others. The ad hoc setup is practical in the home when you're connecting computers that are fairly close together—typically within 100 feet when going through walls. In addition, ad hoc is useful when you need to create a temporary network, such as during a meeting in which several people use laptop computers.

The range for WiFi varies depending on the manufacturer of the adapter you use, how many walls are between the network adapters or access point, and how fast you want your network to be. Check the documentation that came with your hardware for more information.

Ad Hoc Network
The computers must be within range of each other to communicate.

Computer with wireless network adapter

Laptop with wireless network adapter

Laptop with wireless network adapter

If you need to connect more than two computers that are more than 100 feet apart, you should consider setting up a WiFi infrastructure network. This type of network is based around an access point that both has a wireless adapter and is attached to your Ethernet network. The access point allows for a much greater range than an ad hoc network because each computer with a wireless adapter needs to be within range of only the access point and not within range of the other computers.

Infrastructure Network
Each computer needs to be within range of only the access point
to connect to the other computers on the network.

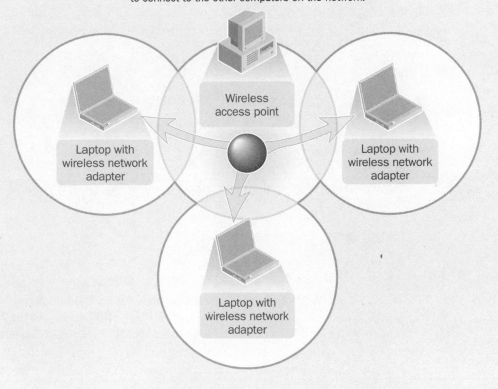

An older standard that is losing ground to WiFi is HomeRF, which is a similar specification that currently offers speeds of 1 Mbps. Another standard you might hear about is Bluetooth, which is designed to create personal area networks (PANs) that allow devices to communicate with each other without wires. For example, if a notebook computer, personal digital assistant, and cell phone all support Bluetooth, each device can communicate with the others simply by being in close proximity.

These three standards are similar in technical design but incompatible with each other. For standards designed for home networking, WiFi offers the fastest connection speed. HomeRF is more affordable but slower than WiFi. Bluetooth is designed only for PANs, and it won't reach the mass market until sometime in 2002.

Another type of wireless connection uses infrared instead of radio waves. The practical use of infrared is fairly limited because the speed is slow and the computers must be in each other's line of sight to communicate.

Tip

Windows XP provides great new tools that make networking with WiFi easy. Its automatic wireless network configuration supports WiFi networking and takes all the guesswork out of configuring a wireless network. After you turn on automatic wireless network configuration, Windows XP detects available wireless networks and sets them up. For more information, in the Windows XP Help and Support Center (accessible by clicking Help And Support on the Start menu), search for *Wireless*.

Using a Phoneline Network

Your home might already have many telephone lines running through it, with connection jacks in each room. A phoneline network takes advantage of this existing wiring to connect your computers. This technology is supported and standardized by a group of industry experts called the **Home Phoneline Networking Alliance (HomePNA)**, and it works by taking advantage of the unused bandwidth of the telephone line. Phoneline networks do not interfere with your normal phone service, so you can talk on the phone and use your home network at the same time.

Important

A phoneline network is not the same as a dial-up connection. With a dial-up connection, one computer on your network uses the telephone line to dial in to the Internet. With a phoneline network, each computer on the network is plugged into the phone lines, but they do not actually make any telephone calls. Rather, they use extra bandwidth on the physical telephone wire to communicate with each other. You can have a phoneline network connecting all your computers and a dial-up connection from one of the computers at the same time.

To use your telephone lines for your phoneline network, you do not need to run any new wires or use a **network hub**, but you must make sure that a phone jack is available near each computer you want to network. The only new hardware you need is a phoneline network adapter for each computer and phone cable long enough to go from the computer to the phone jack. Just plug the phone cable into the phone jack near your computer, and then plug the other end into the appropriate phoneline network adapter on your computer, as shown here:

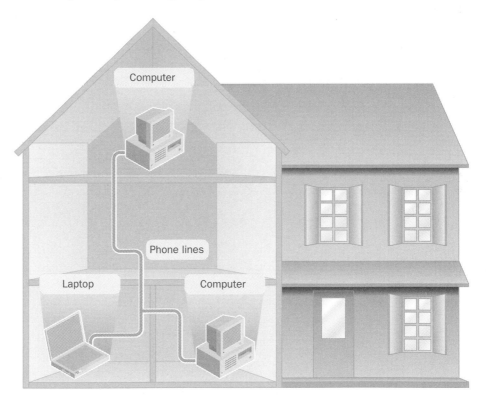

The result is a very convenient and cost-effective home network that can reach speeds of 10 Mbps, which is fast enough for most home users.

Troubleshooting

If you are using a phoneline network and you have multiple telephone numbers in your house, make sure that you plug your computers into phone jacks that all use the same phone number.

Using an Ethernet Network

Ethernet is the most popular type of network connection for businesses and large-scale networks. Ethernet is relatively inexpensive to use and also provides a very fast way for information to travel between computers. There are two types of Ethernet cables: **coaxial** and **unshielded twisted pair (UTP)**. Coaxial cable looks like the type of cable used for televisions, whereas UTP cable resembles a phone cable with an oversized phone jack at each end. You aren't likely to see many coaxial Ethernet networks today, as UTP has become the connection of choice. For networking, you need a type of UTP cable called **Category 5 (Cat5) UTP** or **10/100baseT Cat5**.

A network based on Cat5 UTP cable requires you to have an additional piece of hardware called a **hub**. All the computers on the network plug into the hub, as shown here:

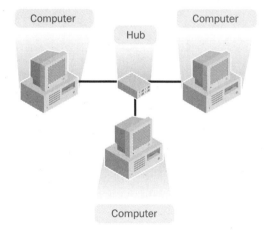

This type of arrangement makes it easy to add computers to or remove them from the network without affecting the existing connections.

The biggest drawback to a network based on Cat5 UTP is the amount of cabling that might be required. If you have several computers spread throughout your home, you might need quite a lot of cables.

Many new homes today are built with Cat5 UTP cables already installed in the walls. This existing wiring can be used to create an Ethernet network. To find out if your home uses Cat5 UTP cable, go to a phone jack and examine the plate. Is the jack a normal **RJ-11 connector**, or does it seem much larger? If the connector looks like an oversized phone jack, as shown on the left, it's probably an **RJ-45 connector**, which is the type of connector used with Cat5 UTP:

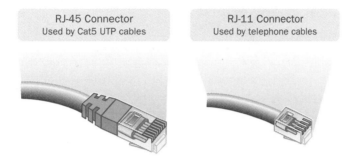

RJ-45 Connector
Used by Cat5 UTP cables

RJ-11 Connector
Used by telephone cables

If your home is wired with Cat5 UTP, ask the builder or installer whether the wiring was installed according to Ethernet installation rules.

Choosing Your Ethernet Speed

When you're shopping for Ethernet cards and hubs, you might notice that Ethernet comes in two speeds: Ethernet and Fast Ethernet. Ethernet can exchange data at 10 Mbps, and Fast Ethernet at 100 Mbps. If you have fewer than eight computers on your network and are using the network to access the Internet or share printers, 10-Mbps Ethernet is the most inexpensive option and is typically fast enough. If you plan to use your network to **stream** music or transfer large files such as graphics, you might want to set up a Fast Ethernet network.

If you can't decide which speed to buy, or if you want to use multiple types of network connections (such as Ethernet combined with phoneline or wireless), consider spending a little extra money for dual-speed Ethernet adapters and hubs that support both 10 and 100 Mbps. Not only will this equipment make it easier for you to upgrade your network in the future, but it will also allow computers with slower network connections to communicate successfully with computers using faster 100-Mbps adapters. Both 10 Mbps and 100 Mbps use the same type of Cat5 UTP cable.

If you don't already have Cat5 UTP cables installed in your home (don't feel bad—we don't either), you still have several options. If your computers are all in the same room, cables can easily be hidden underneath rugs and behind furniture. If your computers are in adjacent rooms, you can drill through walls. If your computers are at opposite ends of your house or on different floors, you might have to run the cables through walls, attics, and crawl spaces. You can hire people to put Ethernet cables in your home, but keep in mind that the farther apart your computers are, the more difficult and time consuming, and therefore the more expensive, it will be to run new wires in your home.

Installing a Network Adapter

To connect to a network, a computer needs a **network adapter**. Network adapters are either internal cards that you install inside your computer or external devices that you connect to one of your computer's unused ports. Newer computers often have network adapters pre-installed; however, you might need to install them yourself. After a network adapter is installed, you can plug the appropriate cables into it to connect the computer to the network.

Internal Network Adapters

An internal network adapter is a **network card** that plugs directly into a slot, called a **Peripheral Components Interconnect (PCI)** slot or an **Industry Standard Architecture (ISA)** slot, inside your computer. Some computers have internal network adapters built in.

Tip

If you use a broadband Internet connection, your computer will need to have two network adapters: one for the Internet connection and another for the home network.

You can tell if your computer already has a network adapter by examining the computer's ports. If you see an RJ-45 **port** in approximately the location shown on the facing page, your computer already has a network adapter installed:

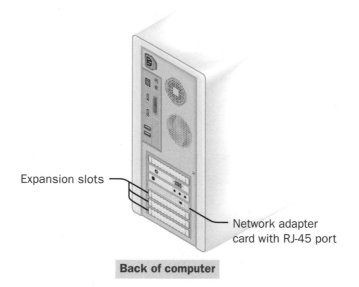

Expansion slots —

— Network adapter
card with RJ-45 port

Back of computer

Before you purchase a network adapter, make sure that your computer has an extra slot, and determine if the slot is PCI or ISA. Newer computers have PCI slots, and some older computers have ISA slots. If you have a choice between slots, always choose PCI because it's more likely that a PCI card will be **Plug and Play compatible**, which means that computer's operating system can recognize the device, making it easier to install and configure it.

Tip

PCI slots are typically white and smaller than ISA slots, which are typically black.

To determine the exact number and type of slots available, you will have to remove the cover of your computer and look inside.

First disconnect the computer from its power source, and then remove its cover. (If you are unsure how to do this, refer to the documentation that came with your computer.) You can then look for an available slot, like the ones shown on the next page, in which to install the network adapter.

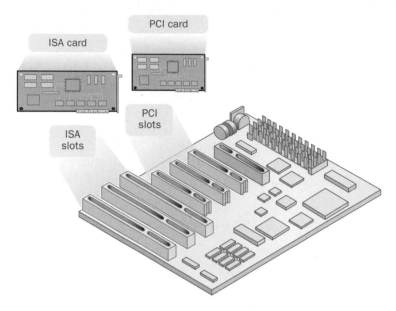

To install your network card, refer to the installation instructions that came with the card. After you've installed the card, replaced the cover, and reconnected the computer, you can turn it back on. At that point, Windows XP detects the new hardware and helps you install any necessary software.

If you use a laptop computer, you can use an internal network adapter that fits into the laptop's **PC Card slot**. These network adapters are about the size of a credit card, except thicker, and they can be installed quite easily. To install a PC Card into your laptop, refer to the installation instructions that came with the card.

Tip

A complete discussion of network adapter installation is beyond the scope of this book. For detailed information about the types of networks and how to install a network adapter, see *This Wired Home* by Alan Neibauer (2nd ed., Microsoft Press, 2000).

External Network Adapters

External network adapters plug into a **serial**, **parallel**, or **USB port** on your computer. The biggest advantage of an external adapter is that you can install it without taking the cover off your computer. However, the disadvantage is that an external adapter can't handle network speeds faster than about 10 Mbps.

If your computer supports USB, you should choose this type of adapter over one with a serial or parallel connection. USB allows for a faster connection, and because USB is Plug and Play compatible, USB devices are very easy to install. Some older computers don't have USB ports, so you should confirm that your computer supports USB before buying the adapter. Look for a port with the USB symbol, like the one shown here:

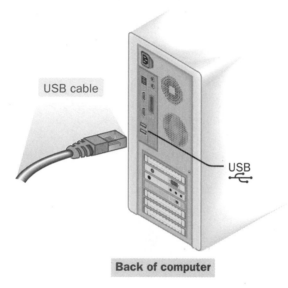

USB cable

USB

Back of computer

See the instructions that come with your USB network adapter for specific installation instructions.

Tip

If you already have devices connected to all the USB ports in your computer, you can purchase a special USB hub that expands the number of available USB ports. Keep in mind, though, that your USB devices must be compatible with the hub.

Using Multiple Types of Networks

What if you want to use a combination of network types, instead of just one? For example, you might have some computers in one room that you can easily connect with Ethernet, but you might also have a laptop with a wireless network adapter that you want to be able to use anywhere in the house. Fortunately, a new feature in Windows XP makes it possible to easily mix and match the types of networks used in your home network, thereby creating a set of linked networks. For example, you can use Ethernet to connect some of your computers and wireless for others.

In the past, setting up a network that mixed different types of technologies was a long, complicated process. If you use Windows XP, however, it's a snap. Windows XP has a technology called a network bridge that makes it possible for data to go from one type of network to a different type of network.

To create a network that uses both wireless and Ethernet—for example, if you already have several computers connected via Ethernet, but you have a laptop with a wireless network adapter that you also want to use on the home network—you simply install both a wireless network adapter and an Ethernet network adapter in the computer running Windows XP. You then configure the network bridge by running the Network Setup Wizard. Or, if you want to configure it manually, use the following steps:

1   On the Start menu, click Control Panel, and then click Network And Internet Connections.

2   Click the Network Connections icon.

3   In the LAN Or High-Speed Internet area, click one of the network connections that you want to bridge, hold down the Ctrl key on your keyboard, and click any other network connections to be included in the bridge.

4   Right-click one of the highlighted network connections, and then click Bridge Connections.

The Network Bridge icon appears, indicating that the bridge is established.

Connecting Two Computers Directly

Sometimes you might want to connect just two computers together to quickly transfer data. Windows XP supports three common ways of making a direct connection:

- *Infrared connection*   This method requires that both computers have **infrared (IR)** ports. This method is a great solution for laptop computers that have built-in IR ports.
- *Direct cable connection*   This method requires a serial or parallel cable.
- *Ethernet*   This method requires Ethernet adapters to be installed in both computers, and an Ethernet crossover cable to connect them.

Before you start making the connection, decide which computer is the **host computer** and which computer is the **guest computer**. (The host initiates the connection with the guest and disconnects from the guest.) You can set up the software for infrared and direct cable connections on Windows XP using the New Connection Wizard, found under Network And Internet Connections in Control Panel.

Tip

If you are using an earlier version of Windows, check Windows Help for specific directions about connecting directly to another computer.

If you need two-way communication and you already have Ethernet cards installed in both computers, you can use an **Ethernet crossover cable**. This is a special type of Ethernet cable that allows two computers to connect directly to each other via their Ethernet network adapters. A direct connection allows you to copy files between two computers without an Ethernet hub. You can set up the software for this type of network using the Network Setup Wizard in Windows XP.

Considering Internet Security

If you plan to use the Internet with your network, you should make sure that your Internet connection is secure from intruders. The way in which you secure your connection depends in part on the way that you connect your home network to the Internet. If you use Windows XP and Internet Connection Sharing to connect to the Internet, the firewall built into Windows XP is your best bet. This **firewall** is turned on automatically when you run the Network Setup Wizard.

Tip

For a detailed description of the various types of online threats and how to guard against them, see the book *Protect Yourself Online* by Matthew Danda (Microsoft Press, 2001).

If you use a non–Windows XP computer to connect to the Internet, you should make sure that the connection is protected by a firewall. This firewall can be either a software application running on the computer that connects to the Internet or a piece of hardware installed between the network and the Internet. A hardware firewall is shown here:

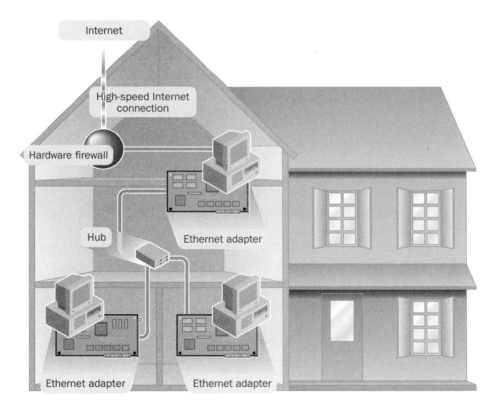

Tip

For more information on using a firewall to secure your connection, see Chapter 5, "Securing Your Home Network."

If you are using a network hub and all your computers connect to the Internet via that hub, you should use a **hardware gateway**. Gateways include a modem and a firewall in one box, so your home network is protected from intrusions as shown here:

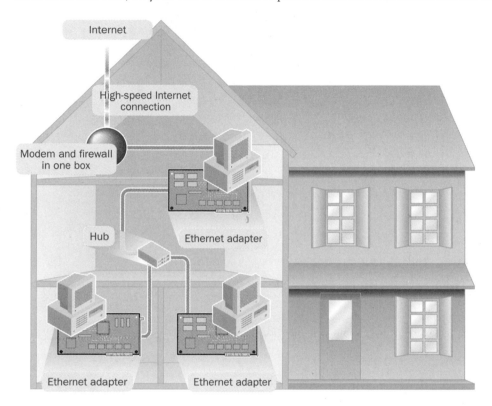

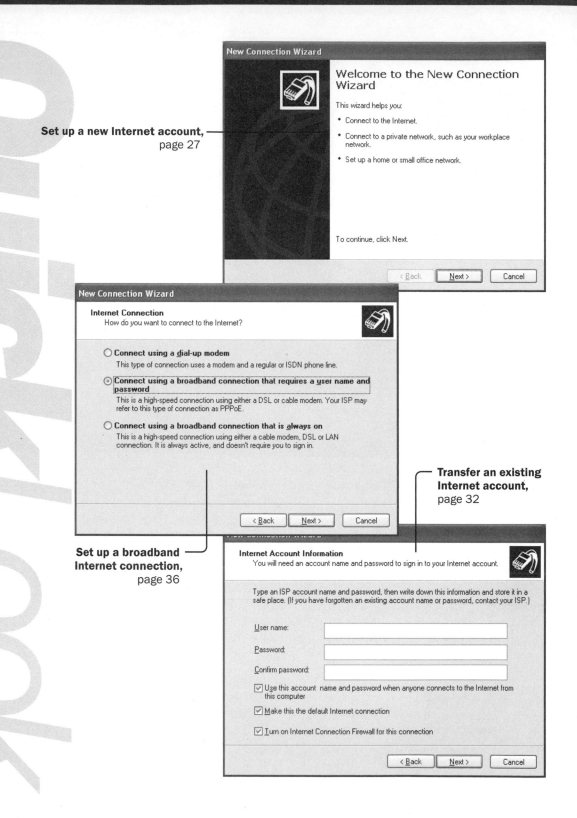

Set up a new Internet account, page 27

New Connection Wizard

Welcome to the New Connection Wizard

This wizard helps you:

* Connect to the Internet.

* Connect to a private network, such as your workplace network.

* Set up a home or small office network.

To continue, click Next.

< Back   Next >   Cancel

New Connection Wizard

Internet Connection
How do you want to connect to the Internet?

○ **Connect using a dial-up modem**
This type of connection uses a modem and a regular or ISDN phone line.

⊙ **Connect using a broadband connection that requires a user name and password**
This is a high-speed connection using either a DSL or cable modem. Your ISP may refer to this type of connection as PPPoE.

○ **Connect using a broadband connection that is always on**
This is a high-speed connection using either a cable modem, DSL or LAN connection. It is always active, and doesn't require you to sign in.

< Back   Next >   Cancel

Set up a broadband Internet connection, page 36

Transfer an existing Internet account, page 32

Internet Account Information
You will need an account name and password to sign in to your Internet account.

Type an ISP account name and password, then write down this information and store it in a safe place. (If you have forgotten an existing account name or password, contact your ISP.)

User name:

Password:

Confirm password:

☑ Use this account name and password when anyone connects to the Internet from this computer

☑ Make this the default Internet connection

☑ Turn on Internet Connection Firewall for this connection

< Back   Next >   Cancel

Chapter 3
Connecting to the Internet

After completing this chapter, you will be able to:

✔   **Set up a new Internet account**

✔   **Transfer an existing Internet account**

✔   **Set up a broadband Internet connection**

One of the most compelling reasons for setting up a network is to share a single Internet connection among multiple computers. The first step in this process—even before configuring the network itself—is to set up the Internet connection. If you have a Microsoft Windows XP computer on your home network, you should make sure that this is the computer that connects to the Internet. This way, you can take advantage of the powerful and easy-to-use Internet Connection Sharing feature and the security features included with Windows XP.

In this chapter, you will learn how to set up a new Internet account from a Windows XP computer, transfer an existing Internet account to a Windows XP computer, and set up a broadband Internet connection on a Windows XP computer.

To complete the exercises in this chapter, you'll need an Internet account. If you currently have no Internet account, you can get help in setting one up by following the instructions in the "Setting Up a New Internet Account" section, later in this chapter. If your Internet account is a dial-up account, take a moment to learn your user name, password, and access telephone number.

Important

If you are currently using an older version of Microsoft Windows, including Microsoft Windows 98 Second Edition or Windows Millennium Edition (Me), to connect the computers on your home network to the Internet, you should switch to using a Windows XP computer instead. Windows XP provides **Internet Connection Sharing** for sharing an Internet connection, and a built-in firewall to protect computers from certain online threats, such as intruders who might try to gain unauthorized access to your computer over the Internet. Internet Connection Sharing and the Internet Connection Firewall are easy to configure by using the Network Setup Wizard; however, you need to set up your Internet connection before you use the wizard.

Tip

In addition to simply using a Windows XP computer, you can use an external piece of hardware called a **gateway** to connect your home network to the Internet. A gateway also typically takes measures to make the computers on your home network safe from intruders. For example, a gateway can hide information about your network, such as the types of computers on it, from potential intruders on the Internet.

Types of Internet Connections

To connect to the Internet, your computer must establish a connection to an **Internet service provider (ISP)**. You can connect to an ISP in several ways, which can be divided into two main categories: dial-up connections and broadband connections.

Dial-Up Connections

For **dial-up connections**, your computer uses a modem to establish a connection to your ISP over a telephone line. Dial-up is the most common type of connection, although it is also the slowest. Dial-up connections require full use of your telephone line while connected, so you can't make a phone call while your computer is connected to the Internet. If you want to connect to the Internet only occasionally and don't plan on sending or receiving large files such as graphic, video, or music files, a dial-up connection is sufficient.

If you want to connect to the Internet only occasionally, but you might send or receive large files, an **Integrated Services Digital Network (ISDN)** connection may be an attractive option. ISDN connections also use a modem and your telephone line to connect to your ISP; however, an ISDN connection does not prevent you from making phone calls while your computer is connected to the Internet. An ISDN connection is faster than a regular dial-up connection, but slower than a typical broadband connection (described on the facing page). In addition, ISDN connections are typically more expensive than broadband connections and usually require professional installation. An ISDN connection is a good alternative when broadband connections aren't available in your area.

Finally, the third type of dial-up connection uses a **digital satellite system (DSS)** dish to download signals from satellites to your computer. Although DSS connections are faster than dial-up or ISDN connections, they require a dial-up connection to upload information, thus preventing you from making phone calls while your computer is connected to the Internet. Although these connections are an improvement over regular dial-up connections, they aren't as fast or as commonly used as broadband connections.

Broadband Connections

If you are planning to use the Internet frequently to surf the Web, play games, send mail, and receive large files, you might want to consider a high-speed Internet connection, also referred to as a **broadband connection**. The two competing types of broadband connections are **Digital Subscriber Line (DSL)** and **cable**. DSL connections use your phone line to establish a connection with your ISP, but they don't interfere with your ability to make phone calls. Cable connections use cable television cables to establish a connection, but they don't interfere with your cable television service. Both of these types of connections are faster than regular dial-up connections and cheaper than ISDN connections, and they maintain a continuous connection to the Internet. In addition, both require special modems that are typically installed by a professional.

Setting Up a New Internet Account

If you don't have an Internet account yet and would like to sign up with an ISP, the New Connection Wizard will walk you through the process of setting up a new Internet account. If you would like help finding and selecting an ISP, the New Connection Wizard can connect you to the Microsoft Internet Referral Service. The Microsoft Internet Referral Service provides links to several of the most popular national ISPs. The manufacturer of your computer may provide Internet service as well.

Important

The setup process for using a *local* ISP is similar to that for transferring an existing account. If you want to use a local ISP, or if you already have an existing Internet account on another computer on your home network, set up your Internet connection by following the instructions provided in the next section, "Transferring an Existing Internet Account." If you want to set up a broadband connection instead, follow the instructions provided in the "Setting Up a Broadband Connection" section.

In this exercise, you don't have an Internet account, and you'd like some help finding an ISP and connecting to it. You will use the New Connection Wizard to set up a new Internet account. Complete the following steps:

1 On the Start menu, point to All Programs, point to Accessories, point to Communications, and then click New Connection Wizard.

If you have not given Windows XP your location information yet, the Location Information dialog box appears:

2 In the Location Information dialog box, enter your country or region, area code, and any other necessary information, and then click OK.

The Phone And Modem Options dialog box appears.

3 In the Phone And Modem Options dialog box, click your current location, and then click OK.

The New Connection Wizard starts:

4 Click Next.

The Network Connection Type page appears:

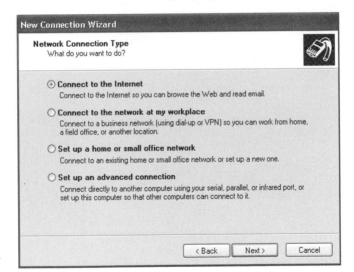

5 Select the Connect To The Internet option, and then click Next.

The Getting Ready page appears:

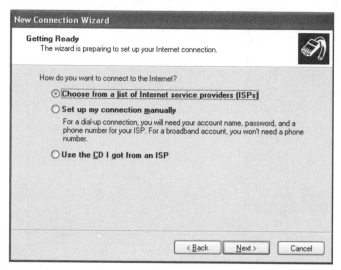

6 Select the Choose From A List Of Internet Service Providers (ISPs) option, and then click Next.

The Completing The New Connection Wizard page appears.

7 In the Select An Option area, select the Select From A List Of Other ISPs option, and click Finish.

The Online Services window appears:

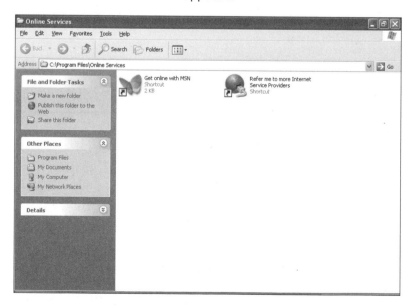

8 In the Online Services window, double-click the Refer Me To More Internet Service Providers icon.

The New Connection Wizard will try to detect your modem; if it can't find it, it will let you choose from a list of modems. If necessary, the New Connection Wizard will set up and configure your modem.

The Step 1 Of 3: Selecting An Internet Service Provider page is displayed.

The New Connection Wizard makes a toll-free call to the Microsoft Internet Referral Service. A list of ISPs is displayed.

9 Click an ISP to find out about billing rates, service information, and speed. Then select an ISP from the list, and click Next.

The Step 2 Of 3: Signing Up With An Internet Service Provider page appears.

10 In the boxes provided, type your name and contact information, and then click Next.

Billing options for the ISP appear.

11 Follow the instructions for choosing a billing plan and providing billing information. When you are finished, click Next.

The New Connection Wizard connects to the ISP and transfers the information.

12 In the User ID box, type a new user name. In the Password and Password (Confirmation) boxes, type a password. Click Next.

A list of access numbers is displayed.

Tip

Keep in mind that the user name and password that you enter on this page are known only to the ISP. They are required only when you attempt to connect to the Internet using that ISP.

13 In the list, select an access number that is close to your home, and click Next.

The terms of the agreement are displayed.

14 Read the terms of the agreement. If you would like to save a copy of the agreement for future reference, click Save Copy. If you agree with the terms, click I Accept The Agreement, and then click Next.

The Step 3 Of 3: Configuring Your Computer page is displayed.

15 In the Name box, accept the default connection name or type a new name for your connection, and click Next.

If you have multiple types of connections set up on your computer, it's helpful to use meaningful names so that you can distinguish between your connections. For example, you could call your MSN account *MSN Dial-up*.

The Completing The New Connection Wizard screen is displayed.

16 To begin browsing immediately, select the check box, and then click Finish.

The Dial-up Connection dialog box appears. The connection information you entered in the wizard is displayed.

17 If you want your password to be entered automatically, select the Save Password check box.

Tip

It's a good idea to select the Save Password check box when you are using Internet Connection Sharing. This makes it possible for other computers on your network to connect to the Internet without first having to go to the Internet Connection Sharing host computer.

18 Click Connect to start your Web browser and connect to the Internet.

19 On the File menu, click Close.

The Auto Disconnect dialog box appears.

20 Click Disconnect Now.

Transferring an Existing Internet Account

If you already have an account with an ISP, you should use the Network Connection Wizard to transfer that account to your Windows XP computer and use the account to establish the connection. This is especially important if you plan to share an Internet connection over your home network, because it allows you to take advantage of the advanced Internet Connection Sharing features included with Windows XP.

Tip

If you signed up with a local ISP, follow the steps in this section to manually set up the account on your computer. If you want to set up a broadband connection instead, follow the instructions in the next section, "Setting Up a Broadband Connection."

To transfer an existing Internet account to your Windows XP computer, you can use the Network Connection Wizard. You will need the following information about your account:

- The phone number you use to access your ISP (for dial-up connections)
- Your user name and password

Tip

If you have your Internet account set up on another computer, you can use the Files And Settings Transfer Wizard to move the account from your old computer to your Windows XP computer. On the Start menu, point to All Programs, point to Accessories, point to System Tools, and then click Files And Settings Transfer Wizard. Follow the wizard's instructions to transfer your Internet settings to your Windows XP computer.

In this exercise, you have an existing Internet account that you'd like to transfer to your Windows XP computer. You've collected the information listed on the facing page, and you're ready to set up the connection. Complete the following steps:

1 On the Start menu, point to All Programs, point to Accessories, point to Communications, and then click New Connection Wizard.

The New Connection Wizard starts.

2 Click Next.

The Network Connection Type page appears:

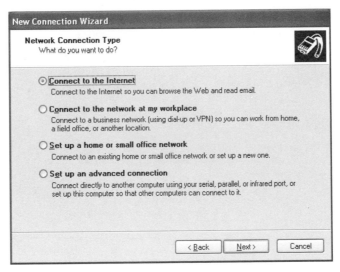

3 Select the Connect To The Internet option, and click Next.

The Getting Ready page appears.

Tip

If you have a CD or floppy disk from your ISP, you can use it to set up your Internet connection. On the Getting Ready page of the New Connection Wizard, click Use The CD I Got From An ISP, and follow the directions on the screen.

4   Select the Set Up My Connection Manually option, and click Next.

The Internet Connection page appears:

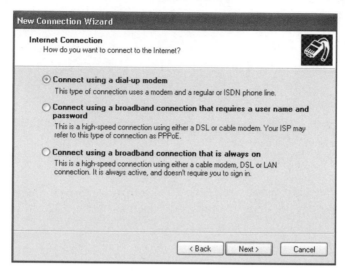

5   Select the Connect Using A Dial-Up Modem option, and click Next.

The Connection Name page appears.

6   In the ISP Name area, type the name of your ISP, and click Next.

The Phone Number To Dial page appears.

7   In the Phone Number box, type the telephone number that your ISP provided you. Click Next.

The Internet Account Information page appears:

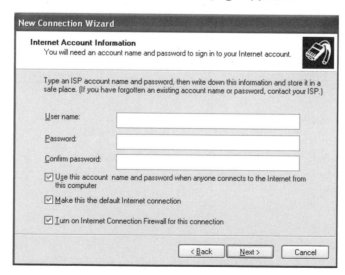

8 In the User Name, Password, and Confirm Password boxes, type the name and password information provided by your ISP. (Simply type your password again in the Confirm Password box; this ensures that you did not accidentally mistype your password.) By default, the three check boxes on the bottom of the screen are selected, indicating that you want to allow any user on this computer to be able to use this account to access the Internet, that this is the default Internet connection, and that the firewall should be enabled. Leave the default settings, and click Next.

The Completing The New Connection Wizard page is displayed:

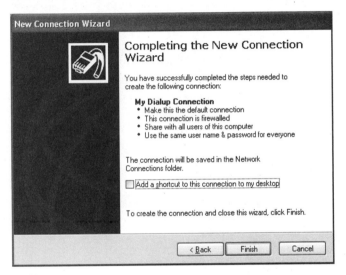

9 Review the settings displayed and click Finish.

10 To connect to the Internet, click Start, point to Connect To, and click the name of the Internet connection you just created.

The Connect dialog box for that connection appears. If you click Dial, Windows XP will automatically dial the ISP and establish a connection.

11 Click Cancel.

Tip

When using a dial-up connection, you can disconnect from the Internet at any time by double-clicking the Internet Connection icon in the Windows taskbar and clicking Disconnect in the Status window.

Setting Up a Broadband Connection

On a Windows XP computer, broadband Internet connections are set up differently than dial-up connections, although you can use the New Connection Wizard to set up your broadband Internet connection as well.

Important

If you use an always-on Internet connection such as DSL or cable, you should protect your computer from hackers and other online threats by using a firewall. Windows XP has a built-in firewall that is set up by default by the Network Setup Wizard.

In this exercise, you have signed up for a broadband Internet account that requires a user name and password, and you have installed the appropriate hardware supplied by your ISP, such as a modem or Ethernet card. To configure Windows XP to connect to the Internet using the broadband connection, complete the following steps:

1   On the Start menu, point to All Programs, point to Accessories, point to Communications, and then click New Connection Wizard.

The New Connection Wizard starts:

2   Click Next.

The Network Connection Type page appears.

3   Select the Connect To The Internet option, and click Next.

The Getting Ready page appears:

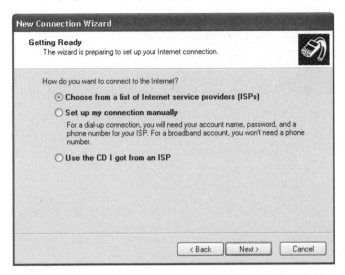

4 Select the Set Up My Connection Manually option, and click Next.

The Internet Connection page appears:

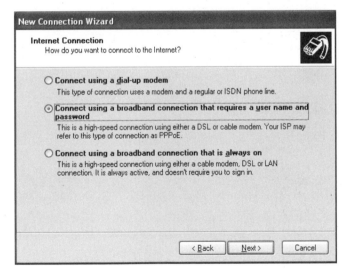

5 Select the Connect Using A Broadband Connection That Requires A User Name And Password option, and click Next.

The Connection Name page appears.

Tip

If your connection is always on—in other words, it is always active and doesn't require you to log on—select the Connect Using A Broadband Connection That Is Always On option, click Next, and then click Finish.

6 In the ISP Name box, type the name of your ISP, and click Next.

The Internet Account Information page appears.

7 In the User Name, Password, and Confirm Password boxes, type the name and password information provided by your ISP, and then click Next. (Simply type your password again in the Confirm Password box; this ensures that you did not accidentally mistype your password.)

The Completing The New Connection Wizard page appears.

8 Review the settings displayed, and click Finish.

9 To connect to the Internet, on the Start menu, point to Connect To, and click the name of the Internet connection that you just created.

The Connect dialog box for that connection appears. If you click Connect, Windows XP will automatically establish a connection.

10 Click Cancel.

Chapter Wrap-Up

If you are continuing to the next chapter:

● Close any open windows.

If you want to delete the Internet account that you created:

1 Click Start, click Control Panel, and then click Network And Internet Connections.

2 Select the Network Connections option. In the Network Connections window, select the icon for the connection you want to delete, and in the Network Tasks area, click Delete This Connection.

3 Contact your ISP to tell it to stop billing you.

Important

Keep in mind that if you plan to connect your home network to the Internet, you should keep your Internet account and use your Windows XP computer to establish the connection.

If you are not continuing to the next chapter:

1 If you want to delete an Internet account that you created, follow steps 1 through 3 on the facing page.

2 If you are finished using your computer for now, on the Start menu, click Log Off, and on the Log Off Windows screen, click Log Off.

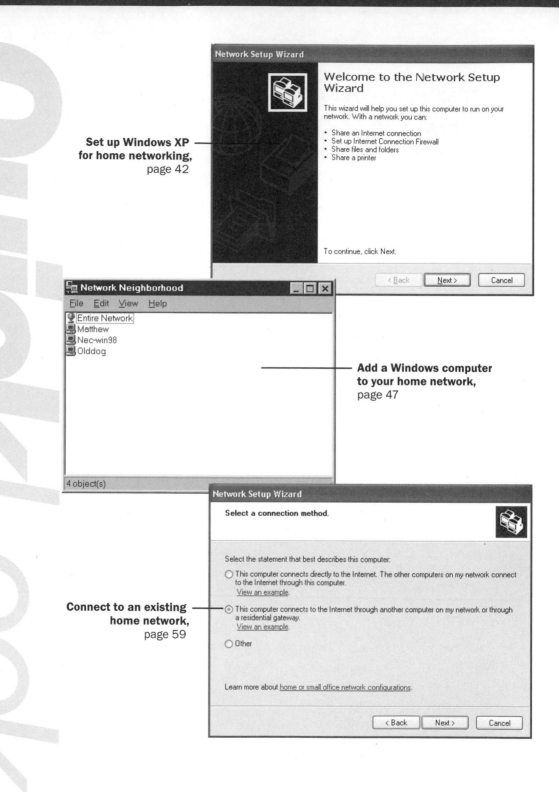

Set up Windows XP for home networking, page 42

Add a Windows computer to your home network, page 47

Connect to an existing home network, page 59

Chapter 4
Installing the Home Networking Software

After completing this chapter, you will be able to:

✔ Configure a Windows XP computer for home networking

✔ Add additional Windows 98, Windows Me, and Windows XP computers to your home network

✔ Add a Windows 95 computer to your home network

✔ Add a Windows 2000 Professional computer to your home network

✔ Add a Macintosh computer to your home network

✔ Set up a Windows XP computer to connect to an existing home network

Now that you've installed your networking hardware and connected to the Internet, you're ready to take the final step to create a home network: installing the home networking software on each computer. Fortunately, the Network Setup Wizard in Microsoft Windows XP makes it easy by automatically configuring your computer to communicate on the network. In addition, you can run the Network Setup Wizard on the other computers that you want to add to your network, including Microsoft Windows 98, Microsoft Windows 98 Second Edition, and Microsoft Windows Millennium Edition (Me) computers. With the help of Windows XP, installing the home networking software and configuring your home network is a snap.

In this chapter, you will learn how to use the Network Setup Wizard to configure a Windows XP computer for home networking and to add additional Windows computers to your home network. You'll also learn how to add a Macintosh computer to your network. Finally, if you already have a home network, you'll learn how to set up a Windows XP computer to connect to an existing network.

To complete the exercises in this chapter, you will need to:

- Install and configure the appropriate network hardware on each computer that you want to add to your network. (For more information, see Chapter 2, "Connecting Your Computers Together.")

- Decide which computer to use as the Internet Connection Sharing host, and set up an Internet connection on that computer. It is highly recommended that you use a Windows XP computer as the Internet Connection Sharing host or a third-party **gateway** that supports Universal Plug and Play (UPnP). (For more information, see Chapter 3, "Connecting to the Internet.")

- Make sure that all computers, printers, and other devices that you want to add to your network are set up and turned on.

- Locate your Windows XP Installation CD-ROM or a blank 3.5-inch floppy disk, and keep it handy.

Setting Up Your Windows XP Computer for Home Networking

The Network Setup Wizard walks you step by step through the process of configuring your network. All you have to do to set up your home network is run the wizard on your Windows XP computer and then run the wizard on each additional Windows 98, Windows Me, or Windows XP computer that you want to add to your home network.

Important

If you want to add a Windows 95 or Windows 2000 Professional computer to your network, you won't be able to use the Network Setup Wizard. Instead, you'll have to configure the settings manually. The steps for connecting each of these operating systems are described later in this chapter.

The Network Setup Wizard helps you to perform the following tasks:

- Configure a Windows XP computer for home networking.
- Add additional Windows 98, Windows Me, and Windows XP computers to the home network.
- Set up Internet Connection Sharing on the network with one computer as the Internet Connection Sharing host.
- Set up a shared folder on each computer on the network.
- Share printers that are attached to computers on the network.

In this exercise, you're setting up a home network using a Windows XP computer and several Windows 98 Second Edition computers. You've connected the computers together using Ethernet network adapters, a hub, and CAT5 UTP cable. You've made sure that all computers on the network are turned on. You've decided to use the Windows XP computer as the Internet Connection Sharing host, and you have already set up an Internet connection on that computer. To use the Network Setup Wizard to set up the Windows XP computer for home networking, complete the following steps:

1 On the Start menu, point to All Programs, point to Accessories, point to Communications, and then click Network Setup Wizard.

The Network Setup Wizard starts:

2 Click Next.

The Before You Continue page appears, listing steps that you need to take before you proceed:

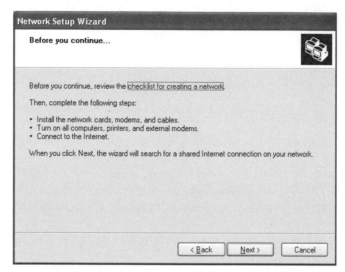

3 Make sure that you've completed the steps listed, and then click Next.

The Select A Connection Method page appears.

4 Select the This Computer Connects Directly To The Internet option, and then click Next.

The Select Your Internet Connection page appears:

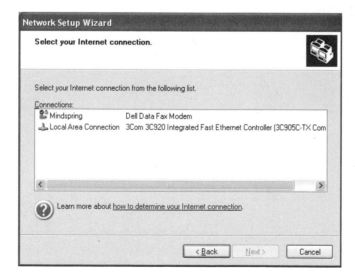

Tip

The options on your screen may be different than those in the examples shown. If you have multiple connections on your computer, there will be several connections to choose from. If your Internet connection is active, Windows XP will highlight the correct connection for you. If your Internet connection isn't active, make sure that you choose the connection that connects your computer to the Internet. This could be a modem or a local area connection (for broadband connections). If you use broadband, make sure you choose the local area connection that connects to your broadband modem.

Important

Keep in mind that for other computers on the network to be able to access the Internet through Internet Connection Sharing, the Internet Connection Sharing host must be turned on.

5　Select your Internet connection in the list, and click Next.

　　The Give This Computer A Description And Name page appears.

6　In the Computer Description box, type a short description of your computer (such as *Family Room Computer*), and in the Computer Name box, type a name (such as *Heather* or *Basement Office*), and then click Next.

　　The Name Your Network page appears.

7　In the Workgroup Name box, leave the default name, and click Next.

　　The Ready To Apply Network Settings page appears:

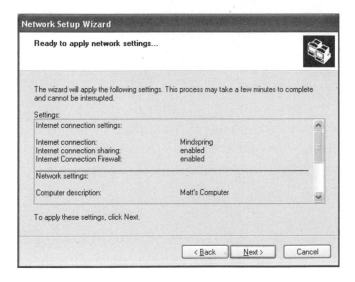

8 Review the settings listed, and then click Next.

The wizard configures the computer for home networking, including turning on the Internet firewall, sharing the Internet connection, sharing any printers connected to the computer, and sharing the computer's Shared Documents folder. This may take a moment. When the wizard is finished, the You're Almost Done page appears:

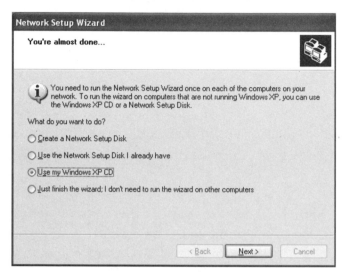

Tip

You can use a floppy disk instead of the Windows XP CD to run the Network Setup Wizard on the other computers on your network. To create a Network Setup Disk, select the Create A Network Setup Disk option on the You're Almost Done page. If you want to create a Network Setup Disk at a later time, run the Network Setup Wizard again on your Windows XP computer, and select all the same options for the network configuration, except on the You're Almost Done page, select the Create A Network Setup Disk option.

9 Select the Use My Windows XP CD option, and then click Next.

The To Run The Wizard With The Windows XP CD page appears.

10 Review the instructions, and then click Next.

The Completing The Network Setup Wizard page appears.

11 Click Finish to close the wizard.

Your Windows XP computer is now set up for home networking. Next you should use the Windows XP CD to run the wizard on each Windows 98, Windows Me, and Windows XP computer that you want to add to the network.

Adding a Windows Computer to Your Home Network

Once you have used the Network Setup Wizard to set up your Windows XP computer for home networking, you can use the wizard to add any of the following computers to your home network:

- Windows XP
- Windows Me
- Windows 98 or Windows 98 Second Edition

In this exercise, you're setting up a home network using a Windows XP computer and several Windows 98 Second Edition computers. You've connected the computers together using Ethernet network adapters, a hub, and CAT5 UTP cable. You've made sure that all computers on the network are turned on. You've run the Network Setup Wizard on the Windows XP computer, and now you will run the Network Setup Wizard on a Windows 98 Second Edition computer.

Important

If you want to add a Windows 95 or Windows 2000 Professional computer to your network, you won't be able to use the Network Setup Wizard. Instead, you'll have to configure the settings manually. The steps for connecting each of these operating systems are described later in this chapter.

The following steps will work on a Windows 98, Windows Me, or Windows XP computer:

1 Verify that the Windows XP computer that you are using as your Internet Connection Sharing host is turned on.

2 Insert your Windows XP CD into the CD-ROM drive of the Windows computer that you want to add to your network.

The Welcome To Microsoft Windows XP screen appears:

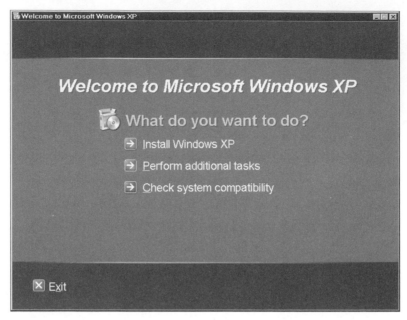

3   In the What Do You Want To Do? list, click Perform Additional Tasks, and then click Set Up A Home Or Small Office Network.

The Network Setup Wizard dialog box appears:

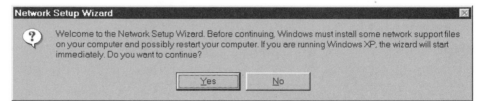

Tip

If you are running the Network Setup Wizard from a floppy disk, insert the disk into the disk drive of the computer that you want to add to the network. On the Start menu, click Run, and then type *a:\netsetup*, and press Enter.

4   Click Yes.

The Network Setup Wizard starts. If you are prompted to restart your computer, remove all floppy disks and CDs from the drives, and then click OK.

5   To restart your computer, click Yes.

The computer restarts, and the Network Setup Wizard appears.

6   In the Network Setup Wizard, click Next.

The Before You Continue page appears, listing steps that you need to take before you proceed.

7   Make sure that you've completed the steps listed on the page, and then click Next.

The Select A Connection Method page appears.

8   Select the This Computer Connects To The Internet Through Another Computer In My Network Or Through A Residential Gateway option, and then click Next.

The Give This Computer A Description And Name page appears.

9   In the Computer Description box, type a short description of your computer, and in the Computer Name box, type a name (such as *Heather* or *Basement Office*), and then click Next.

The Name Your Network page appears.

10   In the Workgroup Name box, leave the default name, MSHOME, and then click Next.

The Ready To Apply Network Settings page appears.

Important

Be sure to give each computer on the network a unique name.

11   Review the settings listed, and then click Next.

The wizard configures the computer for home networking, including sharing any printers connected to the computer and creating a folder called Shared Documents in each user's My Documents folder.

12   Click Finish to close the wizard, and then click Yes to restart your computer.

13   Repeat these steps for each additional Windows 98, Windows Me, or Windows XP computer that you want to add to your network.

Important

If you use a Windows 98 or Windows Me computer, be sure to click OK in the Windows Network Password dialog box whenever you log on to the computer, even if you don't have a password assigned to your user account. If you click Cancel, Windows will start normally, but you won't have access to the network.

Adding a Windows 95 Computer to Your Home Network

The Network Setup Wizard does not support Windows 95 computers. To connect a Windows 95 computer to your home network, you have two options:

- Upgrade the computer to Windows 98, Windows 98 Second Edition, or Windows Me, and then use the Windows XP Network Setup Wizard to connect the computer to the network.
- Manually configure the Windows 95 computer by using the Network dialog box available through Control Panel.

In this exercise, you have already set up your Windows XP computer for home networking. To add a Windows 95 computer to your home network and create and share a folder on the Windows 95 computer's hard disk, complete the following steps:

1 Verify that the Windows 95 computer's network adapter is installed and configured properly and that the computer is connected to the network.

Refer to the documentation that came with the network adapter if you need additional information.

2 On the Start menu, point to Settings, and then click Control Panel.

Control Panel appears.

3 Double-click the Network icon.

The Network dialog box appears. The settings that you see might be different from those shown on the facing page:

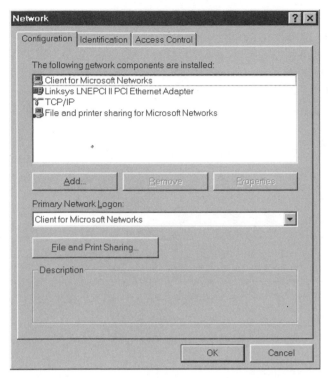

4 On the Configuration tab, make sure that the following network components appear in the The Following Network Components Are Installed list:

■ Client for Microsoft Networks

■ The network adapter used to connect to the network

■ File and printer sharing for Microsoft Networks

■ TCP/IP

To add any of these components, click the Add button. The Select Network Component Type dialog box appears, allowing you to select and add the necessary components.

Tip

To add TCP/IP, in the Select Network Protocol dialog box, click Protocol, click Add, click Microsoft in the Manufacturers list, click TCP/IP in the Network Protocols list, and then click OK.

5 After you've added any required network components, click the File And Print Sharing button.

The File And Print Sharing dialog box appears:

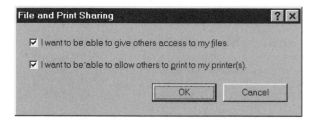

6 Make sure that the I Want To Be Able To Give Others Access To My Files check box is selected, and then click OK.

Tip

If you want to share a printer on your network, you should connect it to the computer that is being used as the Internet Connection Sharing host. In order for other computers on the network to gain access to a shared resource, the computer sharing the resource must be turned on. On your network, the Internet Connection Sharing host is the computer most likely to be turned on and available.

7 Click the Identification tab of the Network dialog box, and type a name and description for the computer. Be sure that the computer name is unique on the network and less than 15 characters long.

8 In the Workgroup box, type *MSHOME*.

If the computers on your home network use a different workgroup name, type that name instead.

9 Click OK to close the Network dialog box.

If you are prompted to insert the Windows 95 CD-ROM, do so. When Windows 95 is finished copying files, you will be prompted to restart your computer.

After restarting your computer, the Enter Network Password dialog box appears, prompting you to type a user name and password to log on to Windows.

10 Make up a user name and type it in. You can either enter a password or leave the password box blank. Click OK.

Important

It is very important that you click OK in the Enter Network Password dialog box. If you click Cancel, Windows will start normally, but you will not have access to the network.

Network
Neighborhood

11 To view the other computers on the network, double-click the Network Neighborhood icon on the Windows desktop.

The Network Neighborhood window appears:

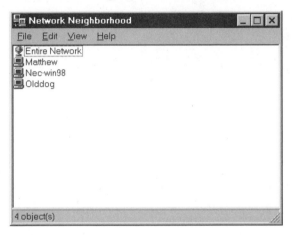

Troubleshooting

If you can't see any other computers on the network, make sure that on the Windows 95 computer, the cables are connected properly, the workgroup name is MSHOME (or whatever workgroup name the other computers on your network are using), and File And Print Sharing is enabled. In addition, try logging off of the computer and logging on again, making sure to click OK instead of Cancel in the Enter Network Password dialog box.

My Computer

12 Double-click the My Computer icon on the Windows desktop.

13 In the My Computer window, double-click the computer's hard disk (probably the drive C).

14 On the File menu, point to New, and then click Folder.

A new folder appears, ready for you to type a name for it.

15 Type *Shared Docs*, and press Enter.

16 Right-click the Shared Docs folder, and click Sharing on the shortcut menu.

The Properties dialog box appears:

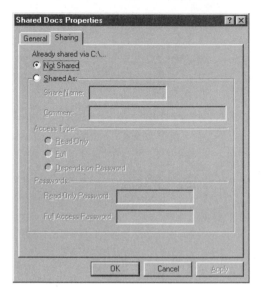

17 On the Sharing tab, select the Shared As option.

18 In the Access Type area, select the Full option, and then click OK.

The icon for the Shared Docs folder now displays a hand under it, indicating that the folder is shared on the network and that other computers can gain access to the files stored on it:

For more information on sharing files and folders on the network, see Chapter 6, "Sharing Data on the Network."

Tip

Your Windows 95 computer can gain access to the Internet through a Windows XP Internet Connection Sharing host. To do this, change the settings of your Web browser so that it will connect to the Internet through the local area network. See the Help file of your Web browser for information about changing how your Web browser connects to the Internet.

Bringing a Laptop Computer Home from Work

If you use a Windows laptop computer at work, you may want to occasionally bring it home and connect it to your home network to share files or print documents. Your computer at work might already be set up for networking, which will simplify this process.

If both your home and office networks are Ethernet networks, you can use the laptop computer's existing network adapter to connect it to your home network. Just attach the Ethernet cable to your laptop's network adapter, and plug the other end of the cable into an available port on your network hub. If you have a different type of home network, such as a home phoneline (HomePNA) network, you can add your laptop computer to the network by first setting up a network bridge. The network bridge that is built into Windows XP makes it easy to connect two different types of networks. In this case, install an Ethernet network adapter on your home Windows XP computer, use it to connect to the Ethernet adapter on the laptop computer (with the appropriate hardware and cables), and then set up the Windows XP network bridge between the Ethernet and the phoneline connection. The network bridge will make sure that the Ethernet network used by your work laptop can communicate with the HomePNA network used by your home network. Network bridges are described in more detail in Chapter 2, "Connecting Your Computers Together."

If the laptop uses Windows 95, Windows 98, Windows 98 Second Edition, Windows Me, or Windows XP and is already set up for a corporate network, you won't need to run the Network Setup Wizard or otherwise change its network settings for it to communicate. Instead, just physically connect it to the network. To gain access to shared folders and files on the network, simply map a network drive or add a new network place (covered in Chapter 6, "Sharing Data on the Network," for Windows XP computers). To use a printer on your network, use the Add Printer Wizard (discussed in Chapter 7, "Sharing Printers and Other Peripherals," for Windows XP computers).

Tip

If you have a WiFi wireless network at home, and you have a wireless card for your laptop computer, Windows XP Professional offers zero configuration networking. This means that if you bring a laptop with a wireless card home from work and take it within range of your wireless home network, your computer will automatically be able to use network resources on your home network.

If the laptop computer runs Windows 2000 Professional, follow the instructions given in the next section.

Adding a Windows 2000 Professional Computer to Your Home Network

Unfortunately, Windows 2000 computers can't be connected to a home network as quickly or easily as Windows XP, Windows 98, Windows 98 Second Edition, or Windows Me computers. The easiest way to connect a Windows 2000 computer to a home network is to upgrade the Windows 2000 computer to Windows XP, and then follow the instructions provided in this book for connecting a Windows XP computer to your network. However, this may not always be an option for you, especially if you plan to connect a computer that you don't own, such as a laptop computer from work, to your network. With some patience, however, you can still connect a Windows 2000 computer to your Windows XP home network. Windows 2000 exhibits the following traits on a Windows XP network:

My Network
Places

- For non–Windows 2000 computers on the network to be able to see shared folders on the Windows 2000 computer, you will have to manually configure each non–Windows 2000 computer to access shared files and folders on the Windows 2000 computer. To do this, on each Windows computer, double-click the My Network Places or Network Neighborhood icon, and then click the Add Network Place icon.

- To access shared folders and printers on your home network, you will have to manually configure the Windows 2000 computer. To add a shared folder, double-click the My Network Places icon on the Windows desktop, and then click the Add Network Place icon. To add a printer, on the Start menu, point to Settings, click Printers, and click the Add Printer icon to start the Add Printer Wizard.

■   To modify certain settings on a Windows 2000 computer, you will need to be able to log on with Administrator privileges. See the sidebar "Logging on as Administrator in Windows 2000" on the following page for more information.

In this exercise, you have brought home the Windows 2000 laptop that you use at work so that you can connect it to your home network. Because the laptop was already set up for the corporate network, you didn't need to change its network settings. Both your home network and corporate network use Ethernet, so you connected the Windows 2000 computer to an Ethernet cable that's plugged into the hub of the home network. Then you shared a folder on the Windows 2000 computer. To set up a Windows XP computer on your network so that it can gain access to the shared folder on the Windows 2000 computer, complete the following steps:

1   On the Windows XP computer on your network, on the Start menu, click My Network Places.

2   In the Network Tasks list, click Add A Network Place.

The Add A Network Place Wizard starts.

3   Click Next.

The Where Do You Want To Create This Network Place? page appears.

4   Click Choose Another Network Location, and then click Next.

The What Is The Address Of This Network Place? page appears.

5   Type the location of the shared folder that you want to access. This should be in the format *computer name**shared folder name* (for example, *Workcomputer**Shareddocs*). Click Next.

The wizard locates the shared folder, and the What Do You Want To Name This Place? page appears.

6   Type a name for the network place (for example, *Shared docs on Work computer*). Click Next.

The Completing The Add Network Place page appears.

7   Click Finish to close the wizard.

The shortcut to the shared folder on the Windows 2000 computer is created. You can now double-click this shortcut to gain access to the shared folder:

Shared docs on Work computer

Logging on as Administrator in Windows 2000

Unlike with Windows 95, Windows 98, or Windows 98 Second Edition computers, you will need to log on to the Windows 2000 Professional computer using an account with Administrator privileges to add a printer, add a network place, or map a network drive. If you are using a Windows 2000 computer from work, you may or may not have these privileges, depending on the network security policy of your employer. If you are unsure whether you have Administrator privileges, ask your company's network administrator.

All Windows 2000 computers have a built-in user account called Administrator that has Administrator privileges. If you know the password for the Administrator account, you can log on and change system settings, including adding a printer, adding a network place, or mapping a network drive. To log on to a Windows 2000 Professional computer with Administrator privileges:

1 Turn on your Windows 2000 Professional computer.
2 Press Ctrl+Alt+Delete to begin.
3 In the User Name box, type *Administrator*.
4 In the Password box, type the Administrator password for your computer.
5 Click the down arrow to the right of the Log On To box, and in the drop-down list, click the name of the computer followed by *(this computer)*.
6 Click OK to log on.
   The Log On To Windows dialog box appears.

Now you can use the Add Printer Wizard on your Windows 2000 Professional computer to access shared printers on your home network. You can also access shared folders on the computers on your home network by mapping drives or adding new network places.

Adding a Macintosh Computer to Your Home Network

What if you have a Macintosh computer that you want to connect to your Windows XP home network? Although you cannot use Windows XP's Network Setup Wizard for this, you can still connect a Macintosh computer to a Windows home network. If you want to use your Macintosh computer only to take advantage of Windows XP's Internet Connection Sharing feature, you do not need to purchase any networking software. Just make sure that the TCP/IP networking protocol is installed on your Macintosh and that your network settings are configured to be automatic. Then configure your Internet browser to use the LAN to connect to the Internet. (See the documentation that came with your Macintosh computer for specific configuration instructions.) If you want to take advantage of shared files or shared printers, you need to purchase a third-party software product such as PC MACLAN or DAVE.

PC MACLAN, from Miramar Systems (*www.miramar.com*), makes it possible for Windows computers to understand Macintosh networking. This is a good solution if you are adding a Windows computer to a predominantly Macintosh network. This approach requires installing the PC MACLAN software on every Windows computer that you want to have access to your Macintosh computers.

DAVE, from Thursby Software (*www.thursby.com*), makes it possible for Macintosh computers to understand Windows networking. This is a good solution if you are adding a Macintosh computer to a predominantly Windows network. This approach requires installing the DAVE software on every Macintosh computer that you want to have access to your Windows computers.

Tip

When combining Macintosh computers and Windows computers on the same network, it is important to remember that some file formats do not work on both computers. For example, there are subtle differences between the Windows version and the Macintosh version of the TIFF format for graphic files, so file conversion is necessary if you want to be able to use a TIFF file on both Macintosh and Windows computers. However, if you have a graphic file in JPEG format, both Windows and Macintosh computers can use it without any conversion. Additionally, files created with Microsoft Word 2002 or Microsoft Excel 2002 can be seamlessly transferred between a Macintosh and a Windows computer. See the documentation that came with your application to find out more about Windows and Macintosh file format compatibility.

Adding a Windows XP Computer to an Existing Windows Network

You can add a new Windows XP computer to an existing home network by simply connecting the computer to the network and then running the Network Setup Wizard. The wizard will walk you through the process of configuring your Windows XP computer for the existing network.

Tip

If your network is using a protocol called **IPX/SPX** instead of **TCP/IP**, you may need to reconfigure your network. The Network Setup Wizard makes this process easy, so you can take advantage of the latest networking technologies to make your home network run seamlessly. Run the Network Setup Wizard on all the computers on your IPX/SPX network to ensure that they communicate in the same language.

However, before you add a Windows XP computer to an existing home network, consider the following questions:

- Does your network have existing network security measures, such as a firewall or gateway, that you would like to continue using?
- Do you already use Internet Connection Sharing on your home network?

If you answered yes to either of those questions, you won't be taking advantage of some of the advanced new features included with Windows XP. Keep in mind that in addition to including a firewall, Windows XP uses a more advanced method for Internet Connection Sharing than previous versions of Windows. As a result, you should make sure that a Windows XP computer serves as the Internet Connection Sharing host for your network. For more information, see the sidebar "Keeping Your Network's Existing Security Features," later in this chapter.

Tip

Windows XP offers a feature called a network bridge, which allows you to seamlessly combine different types of networks. For example, you may want to add computers using a wireless or HomePNA network to an existing Ethernet network. If you attach both types of adapters to your Windows XP computer as described in Chapter 2, "Connecting Your Computers Together," the computer can act as a network bridge, allowing both types of networks to communicate with each other.

In this exercise, you have set up a home network composed of several Windows 98 Second Edition computers. One of the Windows 98 Second Edition computers serves as the Internet Connection Sharing host. You will add a new Windows XP computer to the network, and reconfigure the home network so that the Windows XP computer will be the Internet Connection Sharing host. To turn off Internet Connection Sharing on the Windows 98 Second Edition computer currently serving as the Internet Connection Sharing host, configure its new Internet settings, and then set up your Windows XP computer as the new Internet Connection Sharing host, complete the following steps:

1   On the Windows 98 Second Edition computer that serves as the Internet Connection Sharing host, on the Start menu, point to Settings, and then click Control Panel.

2   Double-click Add/Remove Programs.

     The Add/Remove Programs Properties dialog box appears.

3   Click the Windows Setup tab:

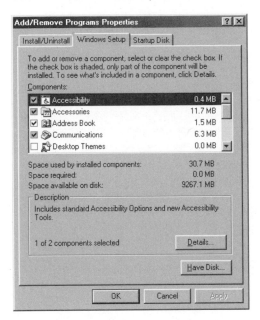

4   In the Components list, select Internet Tools.

5   In the Description area, click Details.

The Internet Tools dialog box appears:

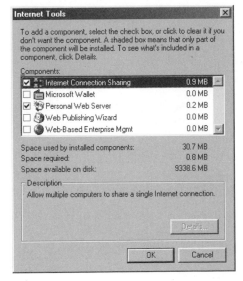

6   In the Components list, clear the Internet Connection Sharing check box.

7   Click OK to close the Internet Tools dialog box.

8 Click OK to close the Add/Remove Programs Properties dialog box.

9 On the Windows 98 Second Edition computer, on the Start menu, point to Programs, point to Accessories, point to Internet Tools, and then click Internet Connection Wizard.

The Internet Connection Wizard starts:

10 Select the I Want To Set Up My Internet Connection Manually Or I Want To Connect Through A Local Area Network (LAN) option, and then click Next.

The Setting Up Your Internet Connection page appears.

11 Select the I Connect Through A Local Area Network (LAN) option, and then click Next.

The Local Area Network Internet Configuration page is displayed.

12 Select the Automatic Discovery Of Proxy Server (Recommended) check box, and then click Next.

The Set Up Your Internet Mail Account page appears, as shown on the facing page:

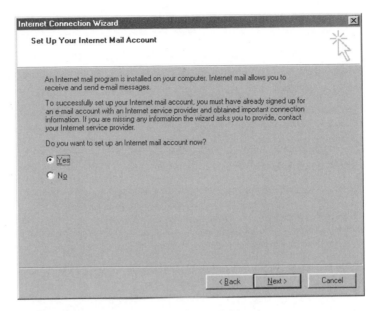

13 Select the No option, and then click Next.

The Completing The Internet Connection Wizard page appears:

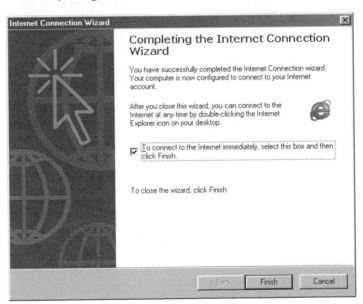

14 Clear the To Connect To The Internet Immediately, Select This Box And Then Click Finish check box, and then click Finish.

15 If prompted, restart your computer.

16 Set up an Internet connection on your Windows XP computer. (See Chapter 2, "Connecting Your Computers Together," for more information.)

17 Verify that your Windows XP computer is physically connected to the network, that all computers on your network are turned on, and that all connected peripherals, such as printers, are turned on.

18 On the Windows XP computer, on the Start menu, point to All Programs, point to Accessories, point to Communications, and then click Network Setup Wizard.

The Network Setup Wizard starts:

19 Click Next.

The Before You Continue page appears, listing steps that you need to take before you proceed.

20 Make sure that you've completed the steps listed on the page, and then click Next.

The Select A Connection Method page appears, as shown on the facing page:

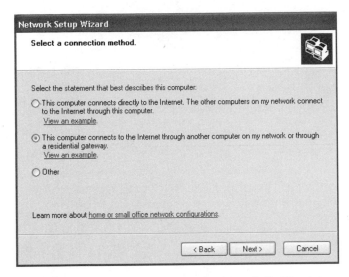

21 Click the This Computer Connects Directly To The Internet option, and then click Next.

The Select Your Internet Connection page appears.

Tip

If you have multiple connections on your computer, there will be several connections to choose from. If your computer is connected to the Internet, Windows XP will highlight the correct connection for you. If your Internet connection isn't active, make sure that you choose the connection that connects your computer to the Internet. This could be a modem or a local area connection (for broadband). If you use broadband, make sure you choose the local area connection that connects to your broadband modem.

22 In the Connections list, select your Internet connection, and then click Next.

The Give This Computer A Description And Name page appears.

23 In the Computer Description box, type a short description of your computer (such as *Office Computer*) and in the Computer Name box, type a name (such as *Heather* or *Basement Office*), and then click Next.

The Name Your Network Page appears.

24 In the Workgroup Name box, type the name of the workgroup that the computers on your local area network are using, and then click Next.

The Ready To Apply Network Settings page appears.

25 Review the settings listed, and then click Next.

The wizard configures this computer for home networking, including sharing your Internet connection, turning on the Internet firewall, sharing printers, and sharing the Shared Documents folder.

When the wizard is finished, the You're Almost Done page appears.

26 Click Next to finish the Network Setup Wizard.

The Completing The Network Setup Wizard page appears.

27 Click Finish to close the wizard.

Important

Keep in mind that for other computers to be able to access the Internet, the computer that's the Internet Connection Sharing host must be turned on.

Keeping Your Network's Existing Security Features

Even though Windows XP comes with a variety of security features (described in Chapter 5, "Securing Your Home Network") and Internet Connection Sharing, you might already have set up a home network with these features. For example, you might have set up a firewall or gateway that you would like to continue using. In addition, although it's not recommended, you might decide to continue using a non–Windows XP computer as the Internet Connection Sharing host on your home network.

To add a Windows XP computer to a network that uses a gateway, run the Network Setup Wizard, and click Next until you see the Select A Connection Method page:

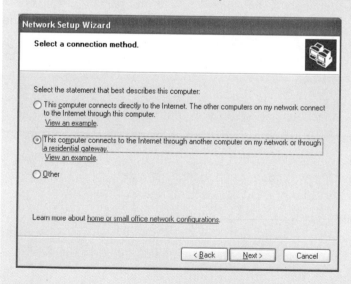

Select the This Computer Connects To The Internet Through Another Computer On My Network option, and click Next. Then follow the wizard's instructions.

Adding Users to Your Windows XP Computer

If more than one person will be using your Windows XP computer, you should create a separate user account for each person. Each user account has the following personalized settings:

- Unique My Documents folder
- List of favorite Web sites
- List of recently viewed Web pages
- Personalized display settings, including wallpaper and screen saver

Tip

Another handy feature of user accounts is fast user switching. When fast user switching is activated, Windows will not close any programs that are running when you log off. This feature is useful if, for example, another person wants to use the computer while you take a short break. When you return to the computer and log back on, your desktop appears exactly as it was before. To turn on fast user switching, on the Start menu click Control Panel, and then click User Accounts. In the Pick A Task list, click Change The Way Users Log On Or Off. Select the Use Fast User Switching check box, and then click Apply Options.

Windows XP allows you to create two types of user accounts, depending on your needs. These accounts are:

- *Computer Administrator* A user with a Computer Administrator account can change any computer settings, install programs and hardware, make system-wide changes, gain access to all private files on the computer, create and delete user accounts, change other users' accounts, change his or her own account type, and change the logon picture associated with the account. The accounts created during the Windows XP setup process are Computer Administrator accounts.

- *Limited* A user with a Limited account can gain access to any program installed on the computer and can change his or her password and desktop settings, but he or she cannot make potentially damaging changes to the computer system. For example, a user with a Limited account cannot install programs and hardware, make system-wide changes, gain access to private files, create and delete user accounts, change other people's accounts, change his or her own account type, or change the picture associated with the account.

In addition, anyone can log on and use your Windows XP computer with a third type of account, **guest**. A user with a guest account can access programs that have already been installed on the computer, but he or she cannot change any system or user account settings. This account is ideal for someone who, for example, needs only temporary access to use the computer to surf the Web but doesn't need to be able to remove or install hardware or adjust user accounts.

Important

User accounts work on only one Windows XP computer. They do not apply to all the computers on your home network. A user account that you create on one Windows XP computer will not automatically be created on other computers on the network.

In this exercise, you're logged on to the Windows XP computer with a Computer Administrator account. You'd like to add an account so that your daughter can use the computer and personalize her settings. To make sure that she can't change any system settings but can still gain access to all the programs installed on the computer, you decide to give her a Limited account. To do this, complete the following steps:

1　On the Start menu, click Control Panel.

　　Control Panel appears.

2　Click User Accounts.

　　The User Accounts screen appears:

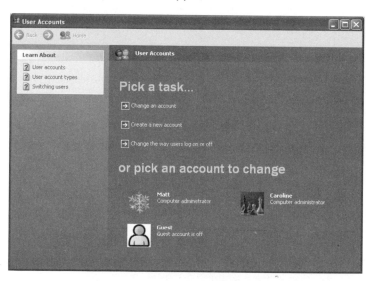

3　In the Pick A Task list, click Create A New Account.

The Name The New Account screen appears:

4 Type a name for the account—perhaps the first name of the person who will be using the account—and then click Next.

The Pick An Account Type screen appears.

5 Select the Limited option, and then click Create Account.

Tip

To improve security on your computer, you can change the Welcome screen so that user names are not shown. This makes it more difficult for an intruder to guess a user name and password and thereby gain access to the computer. It also requires users to know the correct spelling of their user account names as well as their passwords. To change this setting, on the User Accounts screen, click Change The Way Users Log On Or Off. Then on the Select Logon And Logoff Options screen, clear the Use The Welcome Screen check box.

Chapter Wrap-Up

If you are continuing to the next exercise:

● Close any open windows before continuing.

If you are not continuing to other exercises:

● If you are finished using your computer for now, log off Windows.

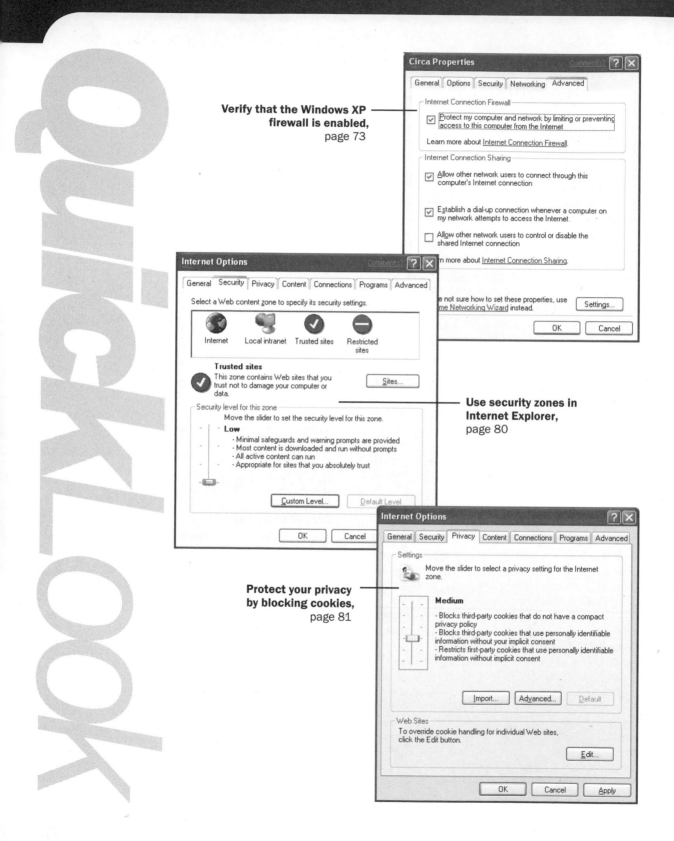

Verify that the Windows XP firewall is enabled, page 73

Use security zones in Internet Explorer, page 80

Protect your privacy by blocking cookies, page 81

Chapter 5
Securing Your Home Network

After completing this chapter, you will be able to:

✔ **Understand how a firewall can protect your home network**

✔ **Verify that Windows XP firewall is enabled on your computer**

✔ **Guard against viruses and other malicious programs**

✔ **Set security zones in Internet Explorer**

✔ **Set privacy preferences to protect your online privacy**

By connecting to the Internet, you're joining an online world in which massive amounts of information are exchanged constantly. While the vast majority of the people and situations that you encounter online will be harmless, there can be oc-casional online threats.

Although it's rare for a hacker to target a specific individual to harass on the Internet, the computer you use to connect to the Internet may still be at risk. Hackers troll the Internet looking for computers with unprotected Internet connections. Once they find one, they can wreak havoc on that computer or enlist it for use in a larger, more elaborate hacking scheme. You can protect your connection by using the **Internet Connection Firewall** that comes with Microsoft Windows XP. This firewall is a software program that protects your computer by shielding it from online hackers.

In addition, **viruses** and other forms of malicious programs are common on the Internet, and if one infects your computer, it can damage any information stored on it. To guard against this threat, you can install anti-virus software and change the security settings in your Web browser.

In this chapter, you will learn how a firewall can protect your computer, and how to verify that the Internet Connection Firewall is enabled on your computer and how to enable it if it's not. In addition, you will learn how to guard your computer against viruses and other harmful programs by using virus protection software and by using security zones in Microsoft Internet Explorer. Finally, you will learn how to set privacy preferences in Internet Explorer to help protect your privacy online.

To complete the exercises in this chapter, you will need a Windows XP computer that is set up as the Internet Connection Sharing host on a home network, and you will need to use Internet Explorer as your Web browser.

Tip

Your configuration of Windows XP might not include Internet Explorer. You'll need to get a copy to complete the exercises in this chapter. You can download it for free from the Microsoft Web site at *www.microsoft.com/windows/ie*.

How a Firewall Works

Computers communicate by sending electronic messages to each other. On the Internet, millions of computers send messages back and forth, so each computer on the Internet has a unique address, called an **IP address**, that's used to distinguish that computer from all the others. When a message is sent from one computer to another, it's divided into small pieces, called **packets**. Each packet contains the IP address of both the sending computer and the destination computer. These packets travel separately through the Internet until they reach the destination computer. Once all the packets arrive, they're reassembled into the original message.

When a computer is connected to the Internet, it constantly sends and receives packets of information. Typically, this information is something useful. For instance, Web browsers receive packets that contain Web pages, and e-mail programs send packets that contain e-mail messages.

Sometimes your computer might receive packets of harmful data. For example, someone might send packets containing a program that scans your computer for weaknesses and then exploits those weaknesses. Other packets might contain malicious programs that can harm your data or steal personal information. To protect your computer from these threats, you should use a firewall to prevent harmful packets from entering your computer and gaining access to your data, as shown on the facing page.

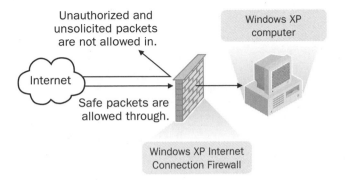

The Internet Connection Firewall included with Windows XP monitors and filters packets that are received by your computer. It prevents outsiders from making unauthorized connections to your computer, and it hides information about your computer from other computers on the Internet. Only the packets of information that your computer has specifically requested are allowed to pass; all others are silently discarded. In addition, the firewall can keep track of attempts to scan or compromise your computer, and it can store that information in log files.

While using the Internet Connection Firewall greatly increases your online security, keep in mind that it is limited to monitoring the Internet connection. It does not scan Internet content, such as Web sites, downloaded files, or e-mail messages, for viruses, nor does it protect your computer from intruders that have physical access to your computer or network.

Tip

For a list of Help topics about how the Internet Connection Firewall works, click Help And Support on the Start menu, and then in the Search box, type *Internet Connection Firewall*, and press Enter.

Enabling the Internet Connection Firewall

The Internet Connection Firewall is enabled when you run the Network Setup Wizard on a Windows XP computer with an Internet connection. You can also enable or disable the firewall by using Network Connections in Control Panel.

Important

If you use Internet Connection Sharing to share your Internet connection with other computers on your home network, it is very important that you use a firewall on the Internet Connection Sharing host computer to protect the Internet connection. This is because all Internet traffic for your network will pass through that computer, and the firewall will help protect all the computers on your home network from online threats. Keep in mind that the Internet Connection Firewall protects only a single Internet connection. If any other computers on your network have modems or can otherwise connect directly to the Internet, those connections won't be protected by the firewall on the Internet Connection Sharing host. If you have computers on your network that can connect to the Internet directly, you should enable a separate Internet Connection Firewall on each of these computers.

In this exercise, you have already set up an Internet connection using a dial-up or broadband connection. You will verify that the Internet Connection Firewall is enabled, learn how to enable it if it isn't already, and learn how to disable it.

Important

The Internet Connection Firewall should not be enabled on any computer that does not connect to the Internet.

Complete the following steps:

1. On the Start menu, point to All Programs, point to Accessories, point to Communications, and then click Network Connections.

   The Network Connections window appears.

2. Right-click the network connection that you use to connect to the Internet, and then click Properties on the shortcut menu.

   The Properties dialog box for that connection appears.

3. Click the Advanced tab, and make sure that the Protect My Computer And Network By Limiting Or Preventing Access To This Computer From The Internet check box is selected. If it is not selected, select it to enable the Internet Connection Firewall.

   The dialog box now looks like this:

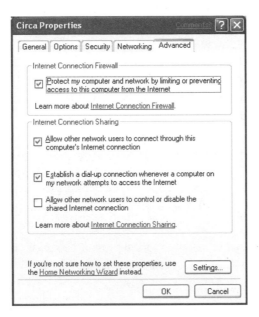

Troubleshooting

The Internet Connection Firewall is designed to stop unsolicited Internet traffic from entering and leaving your computer. However, sometimes it may work too effectively and stop communications that you may otherwise want to go through. To prevent this problem, you can configure the Internet Connection Firewall to allow certain programs or services to have free access through the firewall. For more information, see "Internet Connection Services overview" in Help and Support Center. To open this article, click Help And Support on the Start menu, and then in the Search box, type *Internet Connection Services overview*, and press Enter. A link to the article will appear under *Search Results*.

4 To disable the Internet Connection Firewall, clear the Protect My Computer And Network By Limiting Or Preventing Access To This Computer From The Internet check box.

Important

Customized firewall settings are not transferred from one computer to another. This means that if you have more than one Windows XP computer on your home network that connects to the Internet with Internet Connection Firewall enabled, the firewall settings you define for one computer will not be transferred to the other.

Enabling Security Logging

The Internet Connection Firewall does not display a warning message when it detects unauthorized Internet traffic. Instead, it protects your computer silently. If you want to know how often it has detected and halted attempts at unauthorized communication and what those attempts were, you can configure the Internet Connection Firewall to record its actions in a **log file**.

The log file records information in a standardized format called *W3C Extended Log File Format*. Although it might seem cryptic if you attempt to view it, the log file provides a record of your firewall's behavior that can be of assistance to investigators should anyone successfully break into your computer via the Internet.

To enable security logging:

1 On the Start menu, point to All Programs, point to Accessories, point to Communications, and then click Network Connections.

The Network Connections window appears.

2 Right-click the network connection that you use to connect to the Internet, and then click Properties on the shortcut menu.

The Properties dialog box for that connection appears.

3 Click the Advanced tab of the Properties dialog box, and then click the Settings button.

The Advanced Settings dialog box appears:

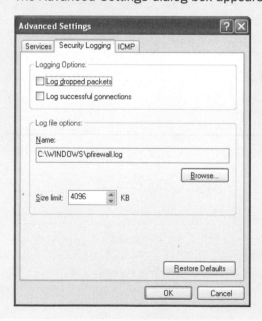

4 Click the Security Logging tab, and then select the Log Dropped Packets check box.

If you are using Internet Connection Sharing to share your Internet connection with other computers on your home network, you can keep track of what services the other computers use on the Internet by selecting the Log Successful Connections check box. For example, when someone on the home network uses Internet Explorer to connect to a Web, the Internet Connection Firewall will create a log entry.

5 In the Log File Options area, make a note of the name and location of the log file. You will need to know this information when you want to view the log file at a later time.

6 Click OK to close the Advanced Settings dialog box.

7 Click OK to close the Properties dialog box.

Now when you connect to the Internet, the Internet Connection Firewall will record actions in the log file. To view the log file, use Windows Explorer to navigate to the file, and double-click the file to open it:

```
pfirewall - Notepad

File  Edit  Format  View  Help

#Verson: 1.0
#Software: Microsoft Internet Connection Firewall
#Time Format: Local
#Fields: date time action protocol src-ip dst-ip src-port dst-port size tcpflags

2001-08-12 08:07:27 OPEN UDP 4.4.182.73 207.46.228.33 1025 123 - - - - - - - -
2001-08-12 08:07:27 OPEN UDP 4.4.182.73 207.46.228.33 123 123 - - - - - - - -
2001-08-12 08:07:28 OPEN TCP 4.4.182.73 64.4.13.212 3023 1863 - - - - - - - -
2001-08-12 08:07:38 OPEN UDP 4.4.182.73 4.2.2.1 3018 53 - - - - - - - -
2001-08-12 08:07:39 OPEN TCP 4.4.182.73 207.46.230.218 3025 80 - - - - - - - -
2001-08-12 08:07:40 OPEN TCP 4.4.182.73 207.46.176.150 3026 80 - - - - - - - -
2001-08-12 08:07:40 OPEN TCP 4.4.182.73 207.68.171.254 3027 80 - - - - - - - -
2001-08-12 08:07:43 OPEN UDP 4.4.182.73 4.2.2.1 3028 53 - - - - - - - -
2001-08-12 08:07:43 OPEN TCP 4.4.182.73 207.68.183.190 3029 80 - - - - - - - -
2001-08-12 08:07:26 OPEN TCP 4.4.182.73 207.46.145.36 3030 80 - - - - - - - -
2001-08-12 08:07:26 OPEN TCP 4.4.182.73 63.162.230.99 3031 80 - - - - - - - -
2001-08-12 08:07:27 OPEN TCP 4.4.182.73 207.46.179.136 3032 80 - - - - - - - -
2001-08-12 08:07:27 OPEN TCP 4.4.182.73 207.46.179.136 3033 80 - - - - - - - -
2001-08-12 08:07:27 OPEN TCP 4.4.182.73 207.68.171.254 3034 80 - - - - - - - -
2001-08-12 08:07:44 CLOSE TCP 4.4.182.73 207.46.176.150 3026 80 - - - - - - - -
2001-08-12 08:07:44 CLOSE TCP 4.4.182.73 207.68.183.190 3029 80 - - - - - - - -
2001-08-12 08:07:44 CLOSE TCP 4.4.182.73 207.46.145.36 3030 80 - - - - - - - -
2001-08-12 08:07:44 CLOSE TCP 4.4.182.73 63.162.230.99 3031 80 - - - - - - - -
2001-08-12 08:07:46 OPEN TCP 4.4.182.73 207.68.183.61 3035 80 - - - - - - - -
2001-08-12 08:07:47 OPEN TCP 4.4.182.73 207.68.182.126 3036 80 - - - - - - - -
2001-08-12 08:07:48 OPEN TCP 4.4.182.73 207.68.182.126 3037 80 - - - - - - - -
2001-08-12 08:07:49 OPEN TCP 4.4.182.73 207.68.183.190 3038 80 - - - - - - - -
```

Keep in mind that the log file will be blank until you connect to the Internet and the Internet Connection Firewall has had a chance to log information.

Protecting Against Viruses

Computer viruses are possibly the biggest security threat to your computer. A **virus** is a small program that sneaks onto a computer, performs some devious task, such as deleting or renaming files, and then spreads to other computers by creating copies of itself. Although viruses have been around almost as long as computers themselves, the Internet has provided them with a new and efficient way to spread.

For example, **Trojan horses** are viruses disguised as normal programs. They have become a popular technique to trick users into unleashing viruses on their computers. Typically a Trojan horse arrives on a computer as an e-mail attachment that appears to be a harmless file or program. Once opened or run, the virus is activated and can wreak havoc on the victim's computer.

To protect your computer and home network from viruses, follow these guidelines:

- Install virus protection software on every computer on your home network.

- Create **backups** of your important files periodically. Store your backups on removable disks, such as CD-RW or Zip disks, and keep the disks in a safe place.

- Never open an e-mail attachment that you were not expecting to receive or from someone that you do not know. (Keep in mind that many viruses send copies of themselves to every user in the victim's address book, so even if you know the sender of an unexpected attachment, check with that person to make sure it is a valid attachment before you open it.)

- Keep your software up to date. Viruses often exploit security holes in software, and software updates frequently include security patches that fix these holes. Use the update features of Windows XP. (See "Using Windows Update" in Help and Support Center.) If you use Microsoft Office products, you should use the Office Update feature periodically. One good resource for current information on keeping your computer secure and your software up to date is the Microsoft Security site at *www.microsoft.com/security.*

- Stay alert for virus warning signs. Look for erratic behavior on your computer and keep tabs on news reports of new viruses. Use the information provided by your virus protection software vendor. Another good source for timely virus information can be found at the CERT Coordination Center at *www.cert.org.*

Important

Be sure to update your virus protection software periodically. Despite your best efforts, however, sometimes a new virus will fool even the most current virus protection software. In that case, your only path to recovery may be to restore your files from backups.

Scanning Your Computer for Viruses

Your best defense against viruses is to purchase commercial **virus protection software**. After it is installed, it will scan your computer for viruses and attempt to eradicate any viruses it detects. Vendors of anti-virus software include:

■ Command Software Systems, at *www.commandcom.com*

■ McAfee, at *www.mcafee.com*

■ Symantec, at *www.symantec.com*

■ Trend Micro, at *www.antivirus.com*

You should install virus protection software on every computer on your home network. At a minimum, you should protect the computer with the most important files and data stored on it.

Important

If you download a file from the Internet, you should always use your virus protection software to scan it for viruses before opening it. If you are unsure how to do this, refer to the documentation that came with your virus protection software for help.

In this exercise, you have already purchased virus protection software and installed it on your Windows XP computer. To use this software to scan your computer for viruses, complete the following steps:

1   On the Start menu, click My Computer.

2   In the Hard Disk Drives area, click Local Disk (C:).

3   In the Tasks area, click Scan For Viruses.

The virus software scans the selected drive for viruses.

Tip

If you detect a virus on your computer, don't panic! Take a moment to consider your options before deciding to undertake drastic measures, such as reformatting your hard disk. If a virus strikes, follow the recommendations of your virus protection software. Sometimes the software can eradicate the virus. Other times, however, your only resort will be to recover your files and data from backups (a great reason to back up your files).

Setting Up Security Zones in Internet Explorer

While you surf the Web, your Web browser is constantly downloading files. Although the vast majority of these files are harmless, occasionally your computer may run across a malicious program. Fortunately, if Internet Explorer is your Web browser, you have a built-in security mechanism for reducing the risk of downloading malicious programs.

Internet Explorer categorizes Internet content into security zones, and each zone is assigned an appropriate level of security. The two general zones with preset security settings are Internet and Local Intranet. The Internet zone applies to content that originates from outside your network, while Local Intranet covers content that originates from within. The default security settings for the Internet zone are much stricter than for the Local Intranet zone. Depending on the specific settings for the zone, Internet Explorer allows files to be downloaded, warns you of the dangers before downloading them, or blocks the files entirely. The two other zones, Trusted Sites and Restricted Sites, allow you to customize Internet Explorer by defining which Web sites you consider to be safe and which you do not.

Important

The Internet Explorer security settings apply only to the computer that you're working on. If you want the settings to apply to all computers on your home network, you will need to manually change the settings on each computer.

The default settings assigned to each security zone are normally appropriate for most users. However, you can change and customize the settings using the Security tab of the Internet Options dialog box in Internet Explorer. Keep in mind that any changes will affect only the computer you're working on and will not be applied to other computers on your network.

To change the settings for a security zone, open the Internet Options dialog box by clicking Internet Options on the Tools menu. On the Security tab, select the zone that you want to customize, and click Default Level. A slider appears that allows you to change the default level of security. The settings are Low, Medium-low, Medium, and High:

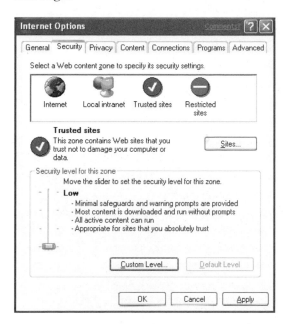

If you have very specific preferences about the type of content that you want to download, you can customize the settings for a security zone. On the Security tab of the Internet Options dialog box, select the zone that you want to customize and click Custom Level. The Security Settings dialog box appears, in which you can set security options for the various types of content that your browser can download.

Protecting Your Privacy

When surfing the Web, you may have noticed that some Web sites remember your personal settings from previous visits. The Web site can do this because it placed a **cookie** on your computer, which is a small piece of data that a Web site can use to identify you as a returning visitor. In general, cookies make surfing the Web a more convenient and enjoyable experience; however, because they can be used to help keep track of your surfing habits, there is a slight tradeoff in privacy and anonymity.

A **first-party cookie** is a cookie placed on your computer by the Web site that you're currently viewing. This type of cookie is typically used to keep track of your user name, password, and other personal settings for that Web site. For security purposes, a Web site can access only the cookie that it placed on your computer, and not cookies placed by other Web sites. However, many Web sites use additional content, such as advertising, from other third-party providers. (You may see this content in the form of advertising banners or pop-up windows.) The third-party provider might also store a cookie, called a **third-party cookie**, on your computer. A third-party cookie poses a greater risk to privacy because it allows the third party to track your behavior on multiple Web sites. For example, if three news Web sites use the same third-party advertiser, the advertiser can use its third-party cookie to track your browsing habits on all three of those Web sites. In general, first-party cookies help make Web sites easier for you to use, while third-party cookies track your online behavior for marketing purposes.

With Internet Explorer version 6.0, you can change your privacy settings to determine how cookies can be stored on your computer. You can set Internet Explorer to warn you when you try to gain access to a Web site that doesn't meet your privacy setting criteria. Additionally, you can set Internet Explorer so that if a Web site posts its privacy policy using the **Platform for Privacy Preferences (P3P) format**, Internet Explorer compares the **privacy policy** with your personal preferences, and determines whether that site's cookies can be stored on your computer. You can define these settings on the Privacy tab of the Internet Options dialog box in Internet Explorer:

Important

For the specific privacy settings to work, the Web site that you visit must use the P3P format to post its privacy policy. Keep in mind that participation in P3P is optional; Web sites are not required to display their privacy policies using the P3P format.

By default, Internet Explorer will block cookies from any Web site that does not display its privacy policy in the P3P format.

Tip

For more information on the P3P format, see the P3P and Privacy on the Web FAQ on the World Wide Web Consortium (W3C) Web site at *www.w3.org/P3P/p3pfaq.html*.

To change your Internet Explorer privacy settings, click Internet Options on the Tools menu to open the Internet Options dialog box, click the Privacy tab, and drag the slider to select a privacy setting. The privacy settings are:

- *Block all cookies*   Prevents all cookies from being saved on your computer, and prevents Web sites from accessing any cookies that may already exist on your computer.

- *High*   Blocks all cookies from Web sites that do not support P3P, and blocks cookies from any Web site that admits in its P3P privacy policy that it uses personally identifiable information without your explicit consent.

Tip

When you click an Agree button, you give explicit consent. When you use a Web site, your use itself gives implicit consent.

- *Medium High*   Blocks third-party cookies that do not support P3P, and blocks third-party cookies from any Web site that admits in its P3P privacy policy that it uses personally identifiable information without your explicit consent. In addition, this setting blocks first-party cookies from any Web site that admits in its P3P privacy policy that it uses personally identifiable information without your implicit consent.

- *Medium*   Same as Medium High, except that it allows restricted access to first-party cookies from any Web site that admits in its P3P privacy policy that it uses personally identifiable information without your implicit consent.

- *Low* Blocks cookies from third-party Web sites that do not have a P3P privacy policy, and when you close Internet Explorer, deletes cookies from third-party Web sites that admit to using information without your implicit consent.

- *Accept all cookies* Allows all cookies to be stored on the computer, and allows Web sites to access any cookies they may have already stored on the computer.

In this exercise, you are using Internet Explorer as your browser, and you'd like to increase your privacy settings. You'll change the default privacy settings from the default, Medium, to High. Complete the following steps:

1 On the Start menu, point to All Programs, and then click Internet Explorer. Internet Explorer starts.

Tip

You do not need to be connected to the Internet to change these settings. If prompted to connect to the Internet when you open Internet Explorer, you can click Work Offline and continue with the steps in this exercise.

2 On the Tools menu, click Internet Options, and then click the Privacy tab.

3 Drag the slider to High:

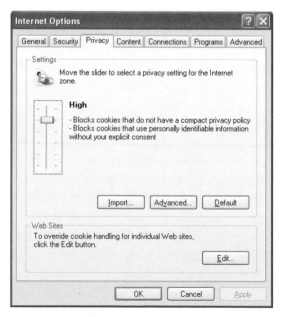

4 Click OK.

Your settings have been changed. Now Internet Explorer will block all cookies that do not support P3P and all cookies from Web sites that admit that they use personally identifiable information without your explicit consent.

Tip

Keep in mind that by increasing your privacy settings and preventing cookies from being stored on your computer, you may not be able to take advantage of some of the features that make Web sites more convenient to use—for example, the ability for certain Web sites to remember your identity and your personalized settings. This reduction in convenience is the tradeoff required to increase your privacy.

Chapter Wrap-Up

If you are continuing to the next exercise:

- Close any open windows before continuing.

If you are not continuing to other exercises:

- If you are finished using your computer for now, log off Windows.

Share a file using the Shared Documents folder, page 88

Share a folder on your Windows XP computer, page 91

Map a network drive, page 107

Share music with other computers using the Media Library, page 96

Chapter 6
Sharing Data
on the Network

After completing this chapter, you will be able to:

✔ **Share a file or folder on your Windows XP computer**

✔ **Share music and pictures on a network**

✔ **Gain access to a shared file or folder on the network**

✔ **Create a shortcut to a folder on the Internet**

✔ **Restrict access to a shared folder or file**

✔ **Map a network drive**

✔ **Stop sharing a folder**

When your computer is part of a home network, it has access to more than just the hardware, software, and files that it contains. This is because each computer on a network can share data with the others. For instance, one computer might store a large set of files, such as a photo album or music collection, and make those files available to every other computer on the network.

You can specify which files on your computer you want to share so that other computers on the network can access them. You can also use your computer to access files and folders that have been shared from other computers. Microsoft Windows XP offers a variety of handy features for sharing files, including a special folder called the Shared Documents folder, which makes it convenient and easy to share documents with others.

In this chapter, you will learn how to share a file by moving it to the Shared Documents folder and how to share an entire folder. You will also learn how to share music and pictures. In addition, you will learn how to use your Windows XP computer to gain access to a shared folder on the network and to create a shortcut to a folder on the Internet. You will also learn how to restrict access to a shared folder and how to map a folder to a network drive so that you can access the folder as though it were stored on a drive on your computer. Finally, you will see how to stop sharing a folder on your computer.

Sharing a File on Your Windows XP Computer

Your network is up and running, and now you're ready to begin using it. One of the most valuable ways of using a network is to share files and folders between computers on your home network. File sharing puts an end to the laborious practice of shuffling files around on floppy disks. You can create and store a document on one computer, and by sharing it on the network, allow someone using another computer on the network to gain access to the file. Some of the ways that you can share files and folders include:

- Using the computer with the largest hard disk as a centralized **file server**. For example, you can store all the photos taken from the family's digital camera.
- Easily transferring large files or groups of files from one computer to another. For example, you may buy a new computer and want to transfer all the existing files to it from your old computer.
- Sharing files and documents between users. For example, you can share a draft of the family trip itinerary on your computer so that your kids can review it later using their computers.

In Windows XP, each user account has a unique My Documents folder, which can store documents, music, pictures—anything at all. You can share or restrict access to the folders in your My Documents folder from other people who log on to your computer.

If you want to share a file or folder with other users on the same computer, you can move or copy it to a **shared folder**. You can designate a folder on your computer to be shared, or you can copy the folder to another folder that's already shared. To make things easy for you, each Windows XP computer has one—and only one—Shared Documents folder. This folder is a centralized storage area that every user of the Windows XP computer has access to. After you run the Network Setup Wizard, the Shared Documents folder is shared on the network. To share a file with other users, both on the computer and on the home network, simply copy it to the **Shared Documents folder**. The Shared Documents folder is convenient for this purpose because it is already shared on the network if you have run the Network Setup Wizard; however, you can easily share any folder on your Windows XP computer.

In this exercise, you have already set up a home network with one Windows XP computer and several Microsoft Windows 98 Second Edition computers. On the Windows XP computer, you will create a new document in your My Documents folder and then move the document to your Shared Documents folder. You will then gain access to that file using a Windows 98 computer on the network.

Tip

If your home network includes Microsoft Windows 95, Microsoft Windows Millennium Edition (Me), or Microsoft Windows 2000 computers, you can still carry out these tasks, but the steps may be a little different from those given here.

To accomplish these tasks, complete the following steps:

1 Log on to the Windows XP computer.

2 On the Start menu, click My Documents.

The My Documents folder appears.

3 On the File menu, point to New, and click Text Document.

A new text document appears in the My Documents folder.

4 Type *Writing Project*, and press the Enter key to give the new document a name.

The Writing Project icon is selected in the My Documents window.

5 In the File And Folder Tasks list, click Move This File.

The Move Items dialog box appears:

6 In the Move Items dialog box, click Shared Documents, and then click Move.

The Writing Project document moves from the My Documents folder to the Shared Documents folder.

Important

Keep in mind that every user on the Windows XP computer has a unique My Documents folder that is available only to that user. However, there is only one Shared Documents folder on the computer, and all users have access to it.

7 In the Other Places list, click Shared Documents.

The Shared Documents folder appears, displaying the Writing Project file. This file is now available to other users, both on the local computer and on the network.

8 Close all programs and windows on the Windows XP computer, but leave the computer on.

9 Log on to a Windows 98 computer on your home network.

Network Neighborhood

10 On the Windows desktop, double-click the Network Neighborhood icon.

The Network Neighborhood window appears, displaying the shared resources on the network:

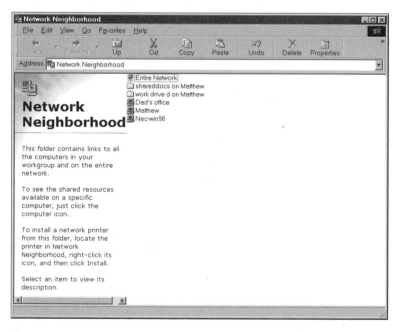

You may have to wait a moment for all the icons to appear.

Tip

If you are using a Windows Me computer, in step 10 you should double-click the icon for My Network Places instead of Network Neighborhood.

11 Double-click the Shared Documents folder that's on the Windows XP computer.

The contents of the Shared Documents folder on the Windows XP computer are displayed.

Tip

By default, the Shared Documents folder on the Windows XP computer is shared on the network with the name *SharedDocs*.

12 Double-click Writing Project to open the file.

The file opens in Notepad. It is blank because nothing has been typed in it yet. You can now edit and modify the file. When you save it, any changes will be saved to the original file on the Windows XP computer.

13 Close Notepad, the Documents window, and all other windows and programs on the Windows 98 computer, but leave the computer on.

Sharing a Folder on Your Windows XP Computer

When you share a folder, you are giving all other computers on the network access to that folder. This is very handy if, for example, one computer stores a collection of pictures or digital music, and everyone on your network needs access to it.

In this exercise, you have already set up a home network with one Windows XP computer and several Windows 98 Second Edition computers. You will now create a new folder on your hard disk, share that folder on the network, and then view the folder on another computer on your home network complete the following steps:

1 Make sure you are logged on to your Windows XP computer with the same account that you used in the previous exercise.

2 On the Start menu, click My Documents.

The My Documents window appears.

3 On the File menu, point to New, and then click Folder.

A new folder appears in the My Documents window.

4 To give the new folder a name, type *Work*, and press the Enter key.

5 In the File And Folder Tasks list, click Share This Folder.

The Work Properties dialog box appears:

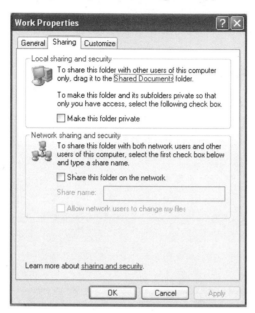

6 On the Sharing tab, in the Network Sharing And Security area, select the Share This Folder On The Network check box.

7 To help other users on the network work with the shared folder, you can assign a name to it. Click the Share Name box, and type *Trip Itinerary*.

Tip

You can restrict access to the shared folder so that others can view the files but not modify them. To do this, in the Work Properties dialog box, clear the Allow Network Users To Change My Files check box on the Sharing tab.

8 Make sure that the Allow Network Users To Change My Files check box is selected, and then click OK. If a warning about long file names appears, click Yes.

The icon for the Work folder now appears with a hand under it, indicating that the folder is shared on the network:

 Work

Troubleshooting

If you do not see a hand under the folder icon, try pressing the F5 key to refresh the screen.

9 Close all programs and windows on the Windows XP computer, but leave the computer on.

10 Return to the Windows 98 computer. Make sure you are logged on with the same account as you were in the previous exercise.

Network Neighborhood

11 On the Windows desktop, double-click the Network Neighborhood icon.

The Network Neighborhood window appears, displaying all the shared resources on the network. You may have to wait a moment for all the icons to appear.

Notice that the Work folder, which you have shared as Trip Itinerary, now appears in the window.

Troubleshooting

If the folder doesn't appear in the Network Neighborhood window immediately, you can view the shared folder by double-clicking Entire Network and then double-clicking the name of the Windows XP computer in the Network Neighborhood window.

12 Close all programs and windows on the Windows 98 computer, but leave the computer on.

Sharing Music on Your Network

Windows XP makes it easy to copy your music CDs to your computer. Once music files are copied, you can listen to music on any of your computers on the network without having to load the CD or copy the music to a different computer.

Tip

You can use the Media Library feature of Windows Media Player to keep track of music stored on other computers so that you can have quick and easy access to it.

You can use Microsoft Windows Media Player to copy music from a CD to your Windows XP computer. To copy music, start by inserting a CD into your computer. The Windows Media Player window appears:

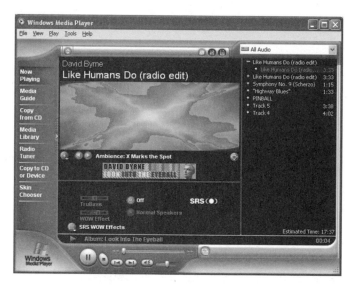

Click Copy From CD in the Windows Media Player window, select the check boxes next to the songs that you want to copy, and then click Copy Music. The music files will then be copied and stored in the My Music folder. (For more information, search for *copying music* in Help and Support Center, and then click "Copying Music From CDs" in the Suggested Topics list.) When you copy a CD using Windows Media Player, it creates folders for the artists and subfolders for albums, all of which are stored in the My Music folder.

Tip

When copying and sharing music, keep in mind that some music may be licensed to prevent illegal distribution. For more information on how Windows Media Player handles licensed digital media, open Windows Media Player Help, search for *license*, and view the topic "Understanding licensed files."

Once files are copied, you can share the music with others on the network. To share the music in the My Music folder, complete the following steps:

1 On the Windows XP computer, click My Documents on the Start menu, double-click the My Music folder to open it, and double-click the folder that contains the album you want to share.

2 Click the album you want to share to highlight the folder.

3 In the File And Folder Tasks list, click Copy This Folder.

4 In the Copy Items dialog box, click Shared Documents, and then click Shared Music.

5 Click Copy.

The music is copied to the Shared Documents folder and is available to other computers on the network. If you want to conserve hard disk space, you can now delete the original copies that are stored in your My Music folder.

Listening to Music Stored on a Windows XP Computer

If you've stored music files in the Shared Music folder on your Windows XP computer, you can listen to it using a different computer on the network. To listen to those music files using a different computer on the network, follow these steps:

1 On a different Windows computer on your network, open the My Network Places or Network Neighborhood window.

2 Double-click the SharedDocs folder on your Windows XP computer to open it, and then double-click the My Music folder to open it.

3 Double-click an album that has been shared in this folder to open it, and then double-click the song you want to play.

Important

Your computer must have a sound card and speakers to play music.

Using Windows Media Player to Add Music Stored on Other Computers

Windows Media Player includes the Media Library feature, which can help you keep track of all the digital media available on your computer. Media Library allows you to have quick and easy access to music stored on your computer as well as music stored on other computers on the network. To add music stored on other computers to your media library, complete the following steps:

1 On the Start menu, click Windows Media Player.

2 In Windows Media Player, click Media Library.

Media Library opens:

Add to Library

3 Click the Add To Library button, and then click Add URL in the drop-down list.

4 In the Open dialog box, click Browse, and then click the My Network Places icon.

5 Double-click the name of the computer from which you shared your music, double-click the Shared Music folder, and then double-click the album you want to add to your media library to open the album.

6   Click the songs that you want to add to your media library to select them, and then click Open.

The songs are added to your Windows Media Player library. As long as the computer that contains your media library is turned on, you can play the songs on any computer on your network.

Sharing Pictures on Your Network

Digital pictures are becoming more and more popular. You may have already acquired quite a collection yourself—for example, from friends and family members who send pictures via e-mail. Or, you may have a **scanner** or **digital camera** that you use to create your own digital pictures.

With Windows XP, it's easy to retrieve pictures from your digital camera. Just attach your camera or **flashcard reader** to your USB port, and Windows XP takes care of the rest. The Windows XP Scanner And Camera Wizard helps you copy pictures from your camera to your Windows XP computer.

Once you've acquired a digital picture, you can share it with others on your network. One advantage of this technique is that you can keep a central, organized repository for your pictures on one computer, and users of the computers on your home network can view the pictures at any time. To share a picture on your network, complete the following steps:

1   On the Windows XP computer, click My Pictures on the Start menu, and then in the My Pictures folder, double-click the folder containing the pictures that you want to share.

Tip

If you don't have any pictures in the My Pictures folder, double-click the Sample Pictures folder to view several picture files that are installed with Windows XP by default.

2   Select the pictures that you want to share. (To select multiple pictures, hold down the Ctrl key as you click.)

The selected pictures are surrounded by heavy frames:

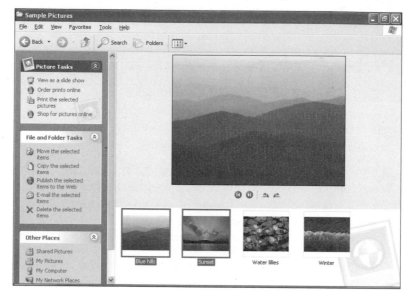

3   In the File And Folder Tasks list, click Copy The Selected Items.

4   In the Copy Items dialog box, click Shared Documents, and then click Shared Pictures.

5   Click Make New Folder, and type *New Pictures* to name the folder.

6   Click the new folder, and then click Copy.

The pictures are copied to the Shared Documents folder and are then available to other computers on the network.

Viewing Pictures Shared on a Windows XP Computer

If one computer on the network has shared some pictures, you can view them using any other computer on your network. To view pictures that have been shared on a Windows XP computer, complete the following steps:

1   On a different Windows computer on your network, open My Network Places or Network Neighborhood.

2 Double-click the SharedDocs folder on your Windows XP computer to open it, and then double-click the My Pictures folder to open it.

3 Double-click the folder in which the pictures are stored, and then double-click the picture that you want to view.

Gaining Access to a Shared Folder on the Network

In the previous exercises, you learned how to share files and folders on a Windows XP computer. Now you'll learn how to use a Windows XP computer to gain access to files and folders that have been shared on other types of Windows computers on the network.

When you need to gain access to a shared folder on another computer, you can browse the network from your Windows XP computer in the My Network Places window. This window displays all the shared computers, printers, and other resources on the network.

In this exercise, you have already set up a home network with one Windows XP computer and several Windows 98 Second Edition computers. To share a folder on a Windows 98 computer and gain access to the shared folder from your Windows XP computer, complete the following steps:

My Computer

1 On the Windows 98 computer, double-click the My Computer icon on the Windows desktop.

The My Computer window appears.

2 Double-click the icon for drive C.

The window displays the contents of drive C.

3 On the File menu, point to New, and then click Folder.

A new folder appears in the window.

4 To name the folder, type *Win98 Example*, and press the Enter key.

Troubleshooting

You may have to right-click the folder and click Rename on the shortcut menu to type a new name for the folder.

5 Right-click the Win98 Example folder, and then click Sharing on the shortcut menu.

The Win98 Example Properties dialog box appears:

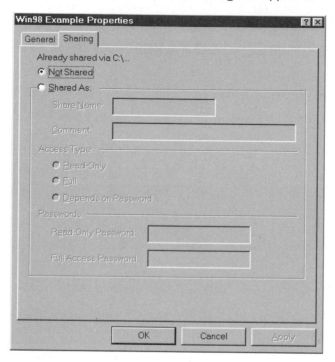

Troubleshooting

If you do not see Sharing on the shortcut menu, you might need to turn on file sharing. On the Start menu, point to Settings, and then click Control Panel. Double-click the Network icon. In the Network dialog box, click File And Print Sharing, make sure the I Want To Be Able To Give Others Access To My Files check box is selected, and click OK.

6 On the Sharing tab, select the Shared As option.

7 In the Access Type area, select the Full option.

Tip

If you are using Windows 95, Windows 98, or Windows Me, you can assign a password to a shared resource. Other users on the network must know the password to gain access. You cannot assign a password if you are using Windows XP or Windows 2000.

8 Click OK to close the Win98 Example Properties dialog box.

The icon for the Win98 Example folder now appears with a hand under it, indicating that the folder is shared on the network:

Win98
Example

9 Close all programs and windows on the Windows 98 computer, but leave the computer on.

10 Return to your Windows XP computer, and make sure you are logged on with the same account as in the previous exercise.

11 On the Start menu, click My Network Places.

The My Network Places window appears, listing all the shared resources on the network.

12 Double-click the Win98 Example folder. (If necessary, click View Workgroup Computers in the Network Tasks list, and then double-click the Windows 98 computer's name.)

The folder is displayed. You can now add to and modify files in this folder just as easily as if they were stored on your Windows XP computer. Because you haven't saved any files in it, the folder is currently empty.

Creating Shortcuts to Folders on Your Network and the Internet

The My Network Places window in Windows XP can do more than just show you what folders are shared from your Windows XP computer and what folders are shared from other computers on your network. It can help you take advantage of storage available from your ISP or folders that you have created on free Web sites or **File Transfer Protocol (FTP)** servers.

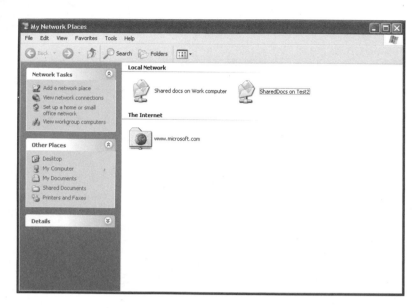

In this exercise, you have already set up a home network with one Windows XP computer and several Windows 98 Second Edition computers. You want to use your Windows XP computer to take advantage of the **Web storage** that is provided for free by your ISP. Your ISP has provided you with a description of its location on the Internet, and the user name and password required to gain access to it. You will use the Add Network Place Wizard to create a shortcut to an FTP site provided by your ISP.

Important

To complete this exercise, you must have FTP server information provided by your ISP, and you must complete the exercise in the section titled "Gaining Access to a Shared Folder on the Network" before continuing with this one.

Complete the following steps:

1   On the Windows XP computer, on the Start menu, click My Network Places.
   The My Network Places window appears.

2   Double-click the Win98 Example folder to open its window.

3   In the Network Tasks list, click Add A Network Place.
   The Add Network Place Wizard appears.

4   Click Next.
   The second page of the wizard appears, asking where you want to create the network place:

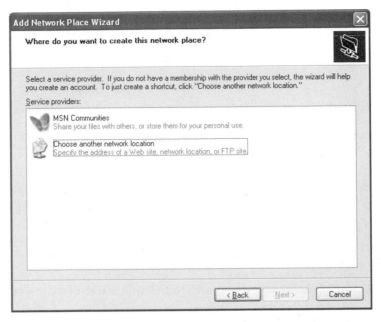

5   Click Choose Another Network Location, and click Next.

The What Is The Address Of This Network Place page appears.

6   In the Internet Or Network Address box, type the location of the FTP site provided by your ISP (such as *ftp://ftp.microsoft.com*), and click Next.

The User Name And Password page appears:

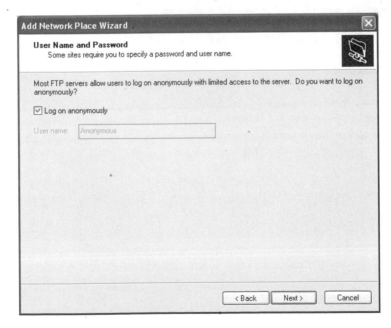

103

7 If your ISP requires anonymous logon, make sure that the Log On Anonymously check box is selected, and then click Next. (If your ISP has supplied you with a user name and password for logging on to the FTP site, clear the check box, and enter that information instead.)

The What Do You Want To Name This Place page appears.

8 In the Type A Name For This Network Place box, type a meaningful name for the connection, such as *FTP to Microsoft*, and click Next.

The Completing The Add Network Place Wizard page appears.

9 Click Finish to complete the wizard.

The folder is displayed in a new window. You can now add to and modify files in this folder just as easily as if they were stored on your Windows XP computer. Any files saved in this folder are stored on your FTP server.

Close

10 Click the Close button to close the window.

The My Network Places window appears. It lists all the shared folders and network places on the network. Notice that the icon for the network place you created appears in the window:

FTP to Microsoft

11 Close all programs and windows on the Windows XP computer, but leave the computer on.

Restricting Access to a Shared Folder on Your Windows XP Computer

If you are using Windows 95, Windows 98, or Windows Me, you can restrict access to a shared folder on the network by assigning a password to it. Windows XP is different. With Windows XP, you can restrict access only to folders that are stored in your My Documents folder. As a result, you should get in the habit of keeping all documents on your Windows XP computer either in your My Documents folder or in the Shared Documents folder.

Any user on any computer is granted full access to files and folders stored in the Shared Documents folder. If you want to have control over how a folder is shared on the computer and on the network, you need to keep it in your My Documents folder. If a folder is in your My Documents folder, you can decide whether to share it completely with others, partially restrict access so that others can view the files but not modify them, or completely restrict access to the folder.

In this exercise, you will continue sharing the Work folder that you created and shared in an earlier exercise.

Important

You must complete the exercise in the section titled "Sharing a Folder on Your Windows XP Computer" before continuing with this one.

To restrict access to it so that other users can view the files within but cannot modify them, complete the following steps:

1 On the Windows XP computer, on the Start menu, click My Documents.

The My Documents window appears.

2 Click the Work folder, and in the File and Folder Tasks list, click Share This Folder.

The Work Properties dialog box appears:

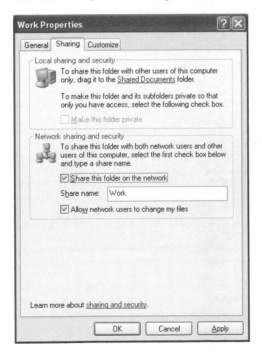

3 Clear the Allow Network Users To Change My Files check box, and click OK.

Now you can add, modify, and delete files in this folder, but other users can only view them.

Keeping Files Private

Windows XP makes it easy to specify which files to share and which to keep private. Files that are in a shared folder are available to others on the network. Files that are not in shared folders are not available to others.

However, keep in mind that other users on the same Windows XP computer may be able to gain access to a folder even if it is not shared on the network. To ensure that the contents of a folder are kept private from other users on the same computer, complete the following steps:

1   Make sure that the folder you want to keep private is in your My Documents folder.

2   Click the folder, and in the File and Folder Tasks list, click Share This Folder.

3   On the Sharing tab of the Properties dialog box, select the Make This Folder Private check box, and click OK.

To ensure that the folder in your My Documents folder is restricted from access by others, keep in mind the following suggestions:

■   Assign a password to your user account. This ensures that no one can log on to the computer using your account, and it prevents users with Limited or Guest accounts from gaining access to your My Documents folder.

■   Make sure the folder is stored on a hard disk formatted as NTFS. Open the My Computer window, right-click the icon for the drive (probably drive C), and click Properties. If the format is not NTFS, search for *NTFS* in Help and Support Center for instructions on converting the format of the drive.

■   Do not share folders that contain private files. Organize your files and folders so that your private files are in folders that are not shared.

■   If a folder that you want to keep private is a subfolder, make sure that none of the folders above it are shared on the network.

■   Verify that the files are private by attempting to access them from another computer on the network and from another account on your computer.

Although these measures are helpful for keeping files private, for true security you should use encryption. Windows XP Professional provides a feature called Encrypted File System (EFS) that can be used to safeguard your files. For more information about EFS, search for *EFS* in Help and Support Center, and then click the "Encrypt File or Folder" topic.

Mapping a Network Drive

The My Computer window displays all the disk drives on your computer and any folders that are shared on your computer. This provides a convenient starting point for gaining access to the information stored on your computer.

If you frequently use a folder that's shared from another computer on the network, you can display that folder in the My Computer window. This is called *mapping a network drive*. When you **map** a shared folder, you assign a drive letter to it, such as E or Z, and it appears in the My Computer window as a new drive. Keep in mind that to gain access to a shared folder that is a mapped drive, the computer that is sharing the folder must be turned on and connected to the network.

In this exercise, you are working on your Windows XP computer and you frequently need access to a shared folder on a Windows 98 computer. You will map the Win98 Example folder so that it appears as drive Z on the Windows XP computer.

Important

You must complete the exercises in the section titled "Gaining Access to a Shared Folder on the Network" before continuing with this one.

Complete the following steps:

1   On the Windows XP computer, click My Computer on the Start menu.

The My Computer window appears.

2   On the Tools menu, click Map Network Drive.

The Map Network Drive dialog box appears:

3 Select a drive letter in the Drive box, such as Z.

4 Click Browse to select a folder.

The Browse For Folder dialog box appears:

5 Under My Network Places, navigate to the Windows 98 computer on your home network. Click the shared Win98 Example folder, and click OK.

The shared folder appears in the Folder box in the Map Network Drive dialog box.

6 Clear the Reconnect At Logon check box, and click Finish.

Important

To gain access to a mapped drive, the computer that is sharing the folder must be turned on and connected to the network.

7 If the My Computer window is not displayed, click My Computer on the Windows taskbar.

The Win98 Example folder now appears as a mapped network drive in the My Computer window:

Network Drives

win98 exampl on 'NEC running Windows 98 (Dad's office)' (Z:)

You can access this folder in the same way that you access other drives and folders on your computer.

Tip

To remove a mapped network drive from the My Computer window, click the drive to select it, click Disconnect Network Drive on the Tools menu, click the drive you want to disconnect in the Network Drives list, and then click OK.

Stopping Folder Sharing

Sometimes you might want to provide access to a folder on your computer for a brief period of time only. When you no longer want to share a folder, it's easy to cut off access to it.

In this exercise, you no longer want others on the network to have access to your shared folders, so you will stop sharing the Work folder on the Windows XP computer and the Win98 Example folder on the Windows 98 Second Edition computer that you shared in a previous exercise.

Important

You must complete the exercises in the sections titled "Gaining Access to a Shared Folder on the Network" and "Restricting Access to a Shared Folder on Your Windows XP Computer" before continuing with this one.

To stop sharing and then delete these folders, complete the following steps:

1   On the Windows XP computer, click My Documents on the Start menu.

The My Documents folder appears.

2   Right-click the Work folder, and click Sharing And Security on the shortcut menu.

The Work Properties dialog box appears.

3   Clear the Share This Folder On The Network check box, and then click OK.

The icon for the Work folder no longer displays a hand under it, indicating that the folder is no longer shared:

 Work

Troubleshooting

If you continue to see a hand under the folder icon, try refreshing the screen by pressing the F5 key.

4 Right-click the Work folder, and click Delete on the shortcut menu to delete the folder.

The Confirm Folder Delete dialog box appears.

5 Click Yes to delete the folder.

6 In the Other Places list, click Shared Documents.

The Shared Documents window appears.

7 Click Writing Project to select it, and in the File And Folder Tasks list, click Delete This File.

The Confirm File Delete dialog box appears.

8 Click Yes to delete the file.

9 Close all programs and windows.

10 On the Windows 98 computer, double-click the My Computer icon on the Windows desktop.

The My Computer window appears.

11 Double-click the icon for drive C.

The window displays the contents of drive C.

12 Right-click the Win98 Example folder, and click Sharing on the shortcut menu.

The Win98 Example Properties dialog box appears.

13 Select the Not Shared option, and then click OK.

14 If the Sharing dialog box appears, notifying you that another user is connected to the folder, click Yes to continue.

The icon for the Win98 Example folder no longer displays a hand under it, indicating that the folder is no longer shared:

Win98
Example

15 Right-click the Win98 Example folder, and click Delete on the shortcut menu to delete the folder.

The Confirm Folder Delete dialog box appears.

16 Click Yes to delete the folder.

Chapter Wrap-Up

If you are continuing to the next exercise:

● Close any open windows before continuing.

If you want to delete the Work and Win98 Example folders:

1 On the Start menu of your Windows XP computer, click My Documents.

2 Right-click the Work folder, and click Delete on the shortcut menu.

3 Click Yes to confirm that you want to delete the folder.

4 Close the My Documents window.

5 On the Windows 98 computer, double-click the My Computer icon on the desktop, and then double-click the icon for drive C.

6 Right-click the Win98 Example folder, and click Delete on the shortcut menu.

7 Click Yes to confirm the deletion.

If you are not continuing to other exercises:

● If you are finished using your computer for now, log off Windows.

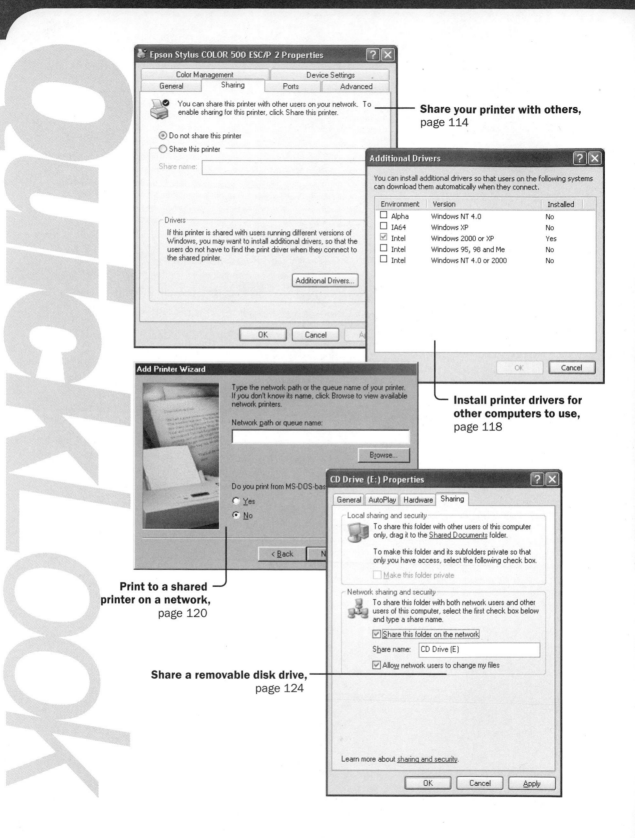

Share your printer with others,
page 114

Install printer drivers for other computers to use,
page 118

Print to a shared printer on a network,
page 120

Share a removable disk drive,
page 124

Chapter 7
Sharing Printers and Other Peripherals

After completing this chapter, you will be able to:

✔ **Share a printer on your network**

✔ **Install printer drivers for other computers to use**

✔ **Print to a shared printer on the network**

✔ **Disable print sharing**

✔ **Share a removable disk drive**

In the past, if you wanted to use a printer that was attached to another computer, you had several time-consuming options. You could install the necessary software on the computer with the printer and then transfer the files that you wanted to print; you could move the printer and physically attach it to your computer; or you could purchase another printer. With a home network, none of these steps is necessary. When you share a printer that is attached to a Microsoft Windows XP computer, you can take advantage of new features that make it easier to install a shared printer on all the computers on the home network.

Similarly, if you would like all the computers on your network to be able to access a removable disk drive, such as a CD-RW drive or a Zip drive, you don't need to purchase and install a separate disk drive on each computer. Instead, you can share the removable drive on the network and allow the other computers on the network to use the drive.

In this chapter, you will learn how to share a printer that's attached to a Windows XP computer. You will also learn how to install **printer drivers** on the Windows XP computer for each type of Windows computer on the network that will be using the shared printer. You will learn how to print to a shared printer using a computer other than the one the printer is attached to, and you will learn how to disable printer sharing. Finally, you will learn how to share a removable disk drive.

Sharing a Printer

Once a printer is attached to and installed on a computer that is already on the network, the printer is immediately shared and can be used by the Windows XP computers on the network. To give printer access to the other computers on your network, you can simply install printers that are shared from your Windows XP computer. This process requires the following two steps:

■ Verifying that the printer attached to the Windows XP computer is in fact shared. (This is in case someone previously stopped sharing the printer.)

■ Configuring the other computers on the network to be able to print to it.

The first step is done for you any time you add a printer to a computer on which you have already run Windows XP's Network Setup Wizard.

The second step involves setting up each computer on the network to print to the shared printer. On Windows XP computers, this step is also done for you. Every time you add a printer to your network, that printer is added to the set of printers that are available for use from your Windows XP computers. For any other computer on your network, you run the Add Printer Wizard and follow the directions for setting up a network printer. The computer can then print to the shared printer in the same way as if it were attached directly to the computer.

Tip

You can share a printer from any type of Windows computer on your network; however, it's recommended that you attach the printer to the computer most likely to be turned on. If you share an Internet connection on your network, the most suitable computer would be the Internet Connection Sharing host, which is typically a Windows XP computer. In addition, Windows XP offers a driver sharing feature that makes it easier to configure other computers to use the shared printer.

In this exercise, you have already set up a home network using one Windows XP computer and multiple Microsoft Windows 98 Second Edition computers, and you will now configure a printer for sharing. For purposes of this exercise, you will not need to physically attach a printer to the Windows computer. Instead, you will walk through the steps of adding a printer using the Add Printer Wizard.

Tip

Normally, when you attach a Plug and Play–compatible printer to a Windows XP computer, you will not need to run the Add Printer Wizard. The computer will automatically recognize and configure the printer.

To set up the printer and then share the printer on the network, complete the following steps:

1   Log on to the Windows XP computer.

2   On the Start menu, click Control Panel.

Control Panel appears.

3   In Control Panel, click Printers And Other Hardware.

The Printers And Other Hardware window appears.

4   In the Pick A Task area, click Add A Printer.

· The Add Printer Wizard appears:

5   Click Next.

The Local Or Network Printer page appears.

6 On the Local Or Network Printer page, make sure that the Local Printer Attached To This Computer option is selected, clear the Automatically Detect And Install My Plug And Play Printer check box, and then click Next.

The Select A Printer Port page appears:

7 On the Select A Printer Port page, leave LPT1 in the Use The Following Port box, and then click Next.

The Install Printer Software page appears.

8 In the Manufacturer list on the Install Printer Software page, click Epson, click Epson Stylus Color 500 ESC/P 2 in the Printers list, and click Next.

The Name Your Printer page appears.

Tip

Keep in mind that these printer settings are used for the purpose of this exercise. When you set up your real printer, use the appropriate manufacturer and printer information for that printer.

9 On the Name Your Printer page, leave the default settings without changing them, and click Next.

The Printer Sharing page appears.

10 On the Printer Sharing page, make sure that the Do Not Share This Printer option is selected, and click Next.

The Print Test Page page appears.

11 On the Print Test Page page, select the No option, and then click Next.

The final page of the Add Printer Wizard appears.

12 Click Finish to add the printer.

An icon for the printer now appears in the Printer And Faxes window:

Epson Stylus COLOR 500 ESC/F
2
0

13 In the Printers And Faxes window, click the printer icon to select it, and in the Printer Tasks list, click Share This Printer.

The Properties dialog box appears for the printer you selected:

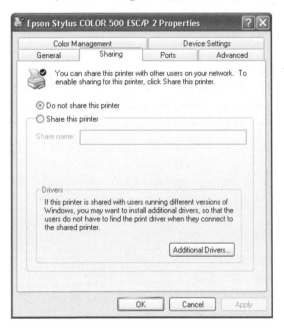

14 On the Sharing tab, select the Share This Printer option.

15 In the Share Name box, type *ColorP* to assign the printer a share name.

The **share name** is the name that other people on the network will see when they connect to the printer. When you complete these steps for sharing your own printer, you should choose a name that will make sense to the other users on your network.

16 Click OK to close the Properties dialog box.

The icon for the printer appears with a hand under it, indicating that it is shared on the network:

Epson Stylus
COLOR 500
ESC/P 2

Tip

You can specify a printer to be the **default printer** so that all print jobs from the computer are automatically sent to this printer. To do this, in the Printers And Faxes window, right-click the printer icon, and click Set As Default Printer on the shortcut menu. The printer icon will then appear with a black check mark, indicating that it's the default printer.

Installing Additional Drivers

For a computer to use a printer, it must have the appropriate printer driver installed. A printer driver is a file that contains information—such as the printer's hardware specifications and internal language—that allows programs on the computer to communicate with a particular printer. As a result, when you install the appropriate printer drivers, one program can easily communicate with a variety of printers.

On a network, each computer that prints to a shared printer must have the printer driver that is appropriate for its operating system. For example, if you have a Hewlett-Packard printer shared on a network composed of Windows XP and Windows 98 Second Edition computers, you'll need one driver for the Windows XP computers and another for the Windows 98 Second Edition computers.

Windows XP can simplify the process of installing printer drivers on the computers on your network by allowing you to store all the drivers on the Windows XP computer. That way, when you run the Add Printer Wizard on the various Windows computers on the network, you don't need to worry about whether you have the correct drivers or where they are located. Windows XP will transfer them to the other computers as needed.

In this exercise, you have already shared a printer on your Windows XP computer, and you are now getting ready to set up your Windows 98 Second Edition computers to print to it.

Tip

You can use the steps in this exercise for Microsoft Windows 95, Microsoft Windows Millennium Edition (Me), and Microsoft Windows 2000 computers.

To simplify the process by installing the Windows 98 Second Edition printer driver on your Windows XP computer, complete the following steps:

1   On the Start menu, click Control Panel, and in Control Panel, click Printers And Other Hardware.

2   In the Pick A Task area, click View Installed Printers Or Fax Printers.

The Printers And Faxes window appears.

3   In the Printers And Faxes window, click the icon for the shared printer to select it, and in the Printer Tasks list, click Share This Printer.

The Properties dialog box appears for the printer you selected.

4   On the Sharing tab, click Additional Drivers.

The Additional Drivers dialog box appears:

5   In the Additional Drivers dialog box, select the Intel Windows 95, 98 And Me check box, and then click OK.

When you follow these steps to set up your own printer on the network, you should select the operating systems that are on the computers that will be using this printer.

The Windows 95, 98 And Me Printer Drivers dialog box appears:

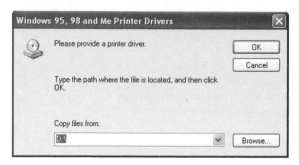

6   In the CD-ROM drive, insert the disk that came with your printer that contains the appropriate drivers.

Tip

You can also download drivers for the printer from the Internet. Typically, you can find the most up-to-date drivers on the printer manufacturer's Web site.

7   In the Copy Files From box, click the disk drive and folder location of the printer driver. If necessary, click the Browse button to browse through all the drives available on your computer.

8   Click OK to install the drivers.

9   Click OK to close the Additional Drivers dialog box, and then click Close to close the printer's Properties dialog box.

Printing to a Shared Printer

After you've shared a printer on the network, you need to set up each computer on your network to be able to print to it. On each Windows computer, simply run the Add Printer Wizard and follow the instructions for adding a network printer. Once the printer is set up, an icon for that printer will appear in the Printers window. The programs on that computer can then print to the shared printer just as if the shared printer were physically attached to the computer.

In this exercise, you have already set up and shared a printer on your Windows XP computer. In addition, you have installed the printer drivers for the Windows 98 Second Edition computers on the Windows XP computer. You will now set up a Windows 98 Second Edition computer so that it can print to the shared printer, and then you'll print a test document on that printer, confirm that the shared printer is set up properly, and print a document over the network using a Windows 98 Second Edition computer.

Tip

With some slight differences, you can use the steps in this exercise for Windows 95, Windows Me, and Windows 2000 computers.

To perform these tasks, complete the following steps:

1   Log on to a Windows 98 Second Edition computer on your home network.

2   On the Start menu, point to Settings, and then click Printers.

The Printers window appears.

3   Double-click the Add Printer icon.

The Add Printer Wizard appears.

4   Click Next.

The next page of the Add Printer Wizard appears.

5   Click the Network Printer option, and then click Next.

The next page of the Add Printer Wizard appears:

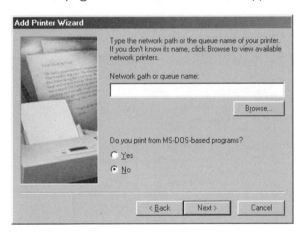

6   In the Network Path Or Queue Name box, type the name and path of the shared printer, and click Next.

For example, to use a printer shared as *ColorP* on the computer called *MATTHEW*, you would type *\\MATTHEW\ColorP*. If you can't remember the name of the printer, you can click Browse to locate the printer on the network.

Windows installs the printer driver.

Tip

Unless you have a very old MS-DOS program installed on your computer and you need to be able to print from it, make sure the No option is selected in the Do You Print From MS-DOS Programs? area.

7 On the next page of the wizard, you can type a name for the printer in the Printer Name box. For this exercise, leave the default name assigned by Windows, and then click Next.

The next page of the Add Printer Wizard appears.

8 Click the No option to tell Windows not to print a test page, and then click Finish.

Windows completes setting up the printer, and an icon for the printer now appears in the Printers window. Notice that the icon appears with a network link on the bottom, indicating that the printer is accessed through the network:

Epson Stylus
COLOR 500

9 Verify that both the Windows XP computer and the shared printer are turned on.

10 On the Windows 98 Second Edition computer, on the Start menu, point to Programs, point to Accessories, and then click WordPad.

The WordPad window opens, displaying a blank document.

11 Type some text in WordPad, such as *Testing the printer from across the network*.

12 On the File menu, click Print.

The Print dialog box appears:

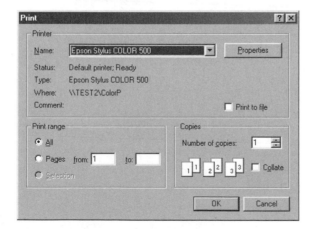

13 In the Name box, click the down arrow, and select the shared printer from the list.

14 Click OK.

The document prints to the shared printer.

15 Close all programs and windows on the Windows 98 Second Edition computer.

Disabling Printer Sharing

You can stop sharing a printer at any time. For example, you might want to print a photo that requires you to load special paper into the printer, and you want to make sure that no one else uses the printer until you are finished. In this case, you would stop sharing the printer, load your special paper, and print the photo using the computer that the printer is attached to. Then when you are finished, you can share the printer again.

In this exercise, you will stop sharing the printer attached to your Windows XP computer. You will also remove the printer from the list of those available to you. To stop sharing the printer and then delete it, complete the following steps:

1 On the Windows XP computer, on the Start menu, click Control Panel, and in Control Panel, click Printers And Other Hardware.

The Printers And Other Hardware window appears.

2 In the Pick A Task area, click View Installed Printers Or Fax Printers.

The Printers And Faxes window appears.

3 In the Printers And Faxes window, click the icon for the shared printer to select it, and then in the Printer Tasks list, click Share This Printer.

The Properties dialog box appears for the printer you selected.

4 On the Sharing tab of the Properties dialog box, select the Do Not Share This Printer option.

5 Click OK.

The icon for the printer no longer displays a hand, indicating that the printer is no longer shared:

Epson Stylus
COLOR 500
ESC/P 2

6 In the Printer And Faxes window, make sure the icon for the printer is selected, and in the Printer Tasks list, click Delete This Printer.

You are asked to confirm that you want to delete the printer.

7 Click Yes.

The printer is removed from your computer, and its icon no longer appears in the Printer And Faxes window.

Sharing a Removable Disk Drive

On a home network, you can share removable disk drives, such as CD, CD-RW, or Zip drives, so that other computers on the network can use them. Sharing a removable disk drive is very handy if you would like all the computers on your network to be able to access a removable disk drive but you don't want to purchase and install a separate drive for each computer. In addition, if there is a certain CD that you frequently use, such as a Microsoft Office installation CD, you can keep the disk in a shared CD drive on an idle computer on your network. Then when you need to access the CD, you don't have to manually track it down and load it into your computer—instead, you can simply access the shared CD drive over the network.

In this exercise, you have a CD that you would like to make available to other computers on the network. To do this, you will share the CD drive from your Windows XP computer, insert the CD that you want to share, and then access the CD from a Windows 98 Second Edition computer over the network.

Tip

You can also use these steps to access the drive from Windows 95, Windows Me, or Windows 2000 computers.

Complete the following steps:

1 On the Windows XP computer, on the Start menu, click My Computer.

The My Computer window appears.

2 In the My Computer window, right-click the CD drive in the Devices With Removable Storage area, and then click Sharing And Security on the shortcut menu.

The CD Drive Properties dialog box appears.

Tip

If you have never shared a storage device before, you might first need to click the If You Understand The Risk But Still Want To Share The Root Of The Drive Click Here link.

3 On the Sharing tab, in the Network Sharing And Security area, select the Share This Folder On The Network check box:

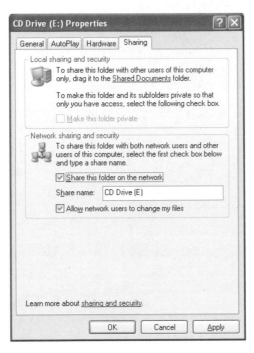

4 In the Share Name box, type the name of the drive, such as *CD Drive*, and then click OK.

The CD drive is now shared.

Tip

To stop sharing a removable drive, in the My Computer window, right-click the CD drive in the Devices With Removable Storage area, and click Sharing And Security on the shortcut menu. On the Sharing tab, clear the Share This Folder On The Network check box.

5 On the Windows XP computer, put a CD in the CD drive. (It can be any CD.)

6 On the Windows 98 Second Edition computer's desktop, double-click the Network Neighborhood icon.

The Network Neighborhood window appears.

7 Double-click Entire Network, double-click Mshome, and then double-click the name of the Windows XP computer on the network.

8 Double-click the name of the shared CD drive on the Windows XP computer.

The contents of the CD in the shared drive appear in the window.

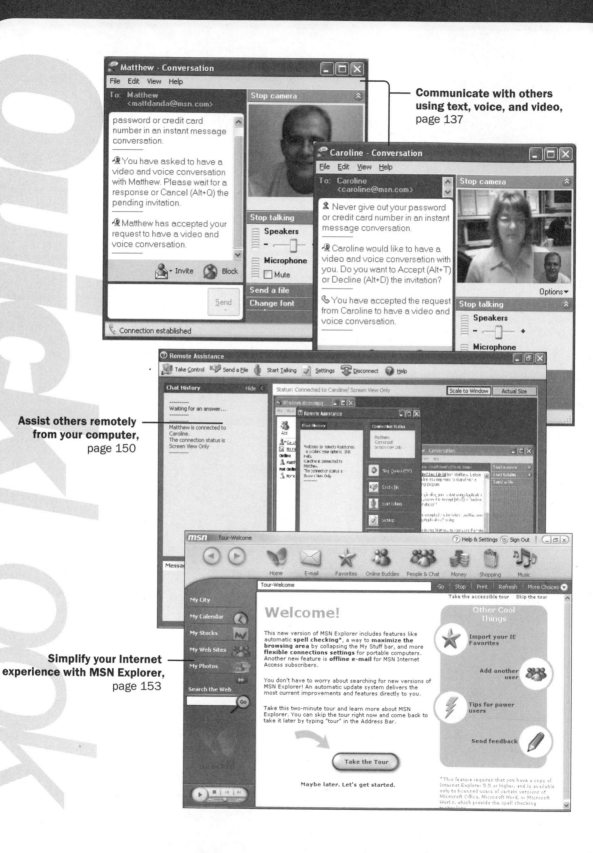

Communicate with others using text, voice, and video, page 137

Assist others remotely from your computer, page 150

Simplify your Internet experience with MSN Explorer, page 153

Chapter 8
Communicating and Collaborating with Others on Your Network

After completing this chapter, you will be able to:

✔ **Use Windows Messenger to communicate via text, voice, video, or e-mail**
✔ **Use Windows Messenger to transfer files and share applications**
✔ **Use Remote Assistance to help another person or allow someone to troubleshoot your computer remotely**
✔ **Simplify using the Internet with MSN Explorer**

Your home network adds great potential to your computing experience—not only inside your house, but on the Internet as well. Now that all the computers on your home network have access to the Internet, everyone in your house can take advantage of the network-enabled programs in Microsoft Windows XP.

One of the powerful tools in Windows XP is the new Microsoft Windows Messenger. With Windows Messenger, you can instantly communicate and exchange data with up to four other people—whether they're in your own home or over a thousand miles away. You can draw pictures and diagrams together on a virtual whiteboard, and you can even share applications or troubleshoot another person's computer remotely.

Another powerful tool is Remote Assistance, which you can use to enlist the help of a friend or colleague in troubleshooting a problem on your computer. Whether you are requesting or giving assistance, you access Remote Assistance through Windows Messenger.

In this chapter, you'll learn how to use Windows Messenger to communicate with others. You'll also use Windows Messenger to exchange files and share an application between computers. You'll use Remote Assistance to troubleshoot another computer from a distance. In addition, you'll learn about MSN Explorer and how it can help you make the most of the Internet.

Using Windows Messenger to Communicate with Others

With Windows Messenger, you can communicate effectively with others by using text, voice, and video. You can send and receive instant messages to and from your friends, speak to each other, and even see each other. You can also have an instant message conversation with up to four other people at once. Windows Messenger is a great way to communicate instantly when people are online. It's faster than e-mail, but it doesn't keep a copy of the correspondence for reference in the future.

With Windows Messenger, you can communicate and collaborate with the people on your **contacts list**. Your contacts list is a list of friends and associates (your contacts, or "buddies") who have agreed to communicate with you. You can add others to your contacts list by clicking the Add button in the Windows Messenger window and then following the instructions provided. You can add a contact to your list if you know his or her sign-in name or e-mail address, such as *person@hotmail.com*.

One powerful feature of Windows Messenger is the ability to get constant updates about each other's online status. You can instantly see who is online and available for conversation, who is online but away from the computer, and who is not online.

In addition to **instant communications**, Windows Messenger is a great **collaboration** tool. Users can send and receive files and work or play together while online with a group of friends or associates.

To participate in a Windows Messenger conversation, you first need to sign up for a Passport. Don't worry—it's free. A Passport provides the unique names or identities that Windows Messenger will use to find you and your contacts and keep you updated with each other's status. A Passport also gives you a simple, secure way to sign in to multiple Internet sites and services with one sign-in name and password. To learn more about the advantages of having a Passport, see the Passport Web site at *www.passport.com*.

Tip

If you have an MSN Hotmail account, you already have a Passport.

Windows Messenger starts whenever you turn on your Windows XP computer. When you connect to the Internet, Windows Messenger connects to the Messenger service, which keeps you and your contacts updated with each other's status and gives you the ability to communicate and collaborate. This service is provided to you for free.

Tip

You can turn off the auto-start feature of Windows Messenger. On the Windows task-bar, right-click the Windows Messenger icon, and click Open on the shortcut menu. On the Tools menu, click Options. On the Preferences tab of the Options dialog box, clear the Run This Program When Windows Starts check box, and then click OK.

When you're signed in, the Windows Messenger icon appears at the right end of the Windows taskbar:

Important

Windows Messenger is not the same as an Internet chat room. With Windows Messenger, you communicate only with the people you want to. Unlike chat rooms, which are often publicized and available to anyone who wants to drop in and participate, the only people who know about Windows Messenger conversations are the people who have been invited to participate. This makes Windows Messenger more personal and private than chat rooms.

Keep in mind that although Windows Messenger offers more privacy than Internet chat, it is not necessarily more secure. You should never send sensitive information, such as your Social Security number or credit card number, when using Windows Messenger or any other **instant messaging** program.

In this exercise, you have a home office that is located in a remote part of your house, and the office includes a Windows XP computer that is connected to your home network. Your spouse is in the bedroom using a networked Windows XP computer and would like to have a quick conversation with you. You will start Windows Messenger on each computer and, if necessary, create Passports for you and your spouse, and you will then add each other as contacts on your respective computers.

Important

You will need two Windows XP computers on your home network to complete the exercises in this chapter.

To communicate using Windows Messenger, complete the following steps:

1 Make sure that both computers are able to connect to the Internet and that the Internet connection is established.

2 On your Windows XP computer, on the Start menu, point to All Programs, and then click Windows Messenger.

3 If you do not already have a Passport, follow the steps for creating a new account. If you have a Passport already, go ahead and sign in.

The Windows Messenger screen appears, ready for you to begin:

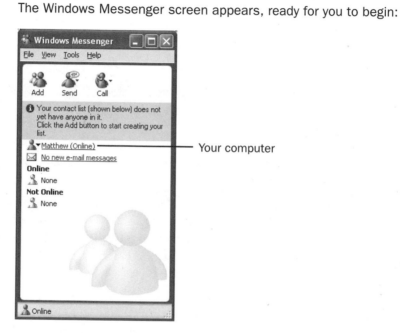

Your computer

Important

If you have children aged 12 and under who want to use Windows Messenger, you might want to get a Kids Passport for them. For more information, see the Kids Passport Web site at *kids.passport.com*.

4 On your spouse's computer, repeat steps 2 and 3 to open Windows Messenger and, if necessary, set up a Passport.

Both computers are now running Windows Messenger:

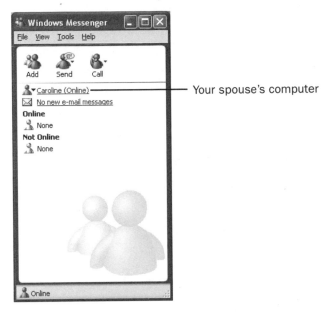

Your spouse's computer

5 On your Windows XP computer, click the Add icon in the Windows Messenger window.

The Add A Contact screen appears:

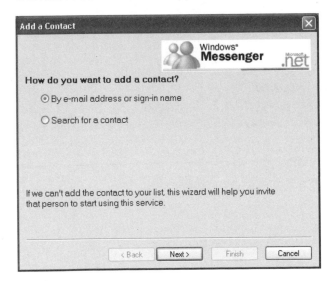

6 In the How Do You Want To Add A Contact? list, select the By E-mail Address Or Sign-In Name option, and then click Next.

The Please Type Your Contact's Complete E-mail Address screen appears.

7 Type your spouse's complete e-mail address in the box provided, and then click Next. If asked what service your contact uses, select the .NET Messenger Service option.

The Success! screen appears:

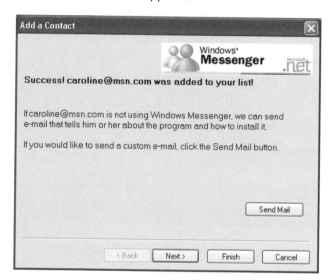

Tip

You can click the Send Mail button to send a customizable e-mail message to the contact that you added. The default text of this message contains helpful information describing the Windows Messenger program and how to use it.

8 Click Next.

The You're Done! screen appears.

9 Click Finish.

The Windows Messenger screen now shows the contact in the Not Online list:

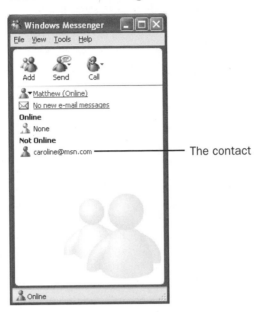

The contact

10 On your spouse's computer, a message appears, indicating that a contact was added:

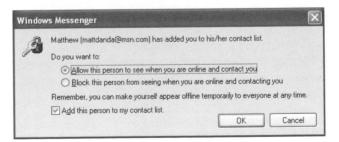

11 Select the Allow This Person To See When You Are Online And Contact You option, make sure the Add This Person To My Contact List check box is selected, and then click OK.

Both computers will now include contacts for each other, which will appear in the Online list of the Windows Messenger window:

Your computer

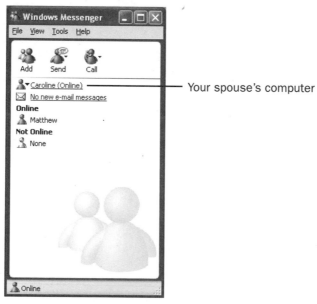

Your spouse's computer

Important

You must be connected to the Internet to use Windows Messenger, even if you are communicating only with computers on your home network.

Send

12 On your computer, click the Send icon in the Windows Messenger window, and click your spouse's name in the drop-down list.

The Conversation window appears. The name in the title bar indicates the person you are communicating with:

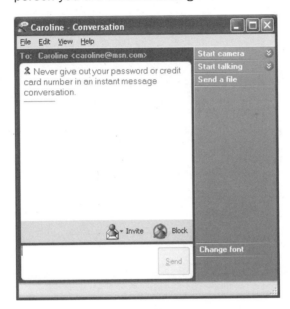

13 Type *Hello there*, and then click Send.

A notification pop-up window will appear on your spouse's computer, containing the message:

14 On your spouse's computer, on the taskbar, click the notification pop-up window or Conversation button to open the Conversation window.

Both computers now have Conversation windows open, and both users can converse instantly by typing messages and clicking Send:

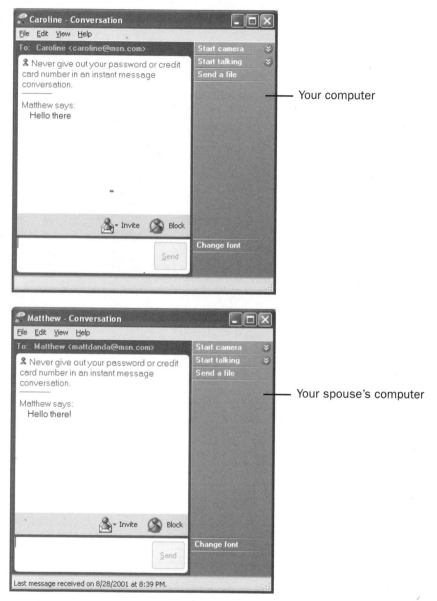

Your computer

Your spouse's computer

15 Close the Conversation window on both computers, but leave Windows Messenger running.

Tip

Once you have initiated an instant message conversation with a contact, you can add more people to the conversation. To invite others, in the message window, click the Invite icon on the bar below the sent message, point to To Join This Conversation, and then click a name. You can have up to four other people (a total of five, including yourself) at one time in a conversation.

Using Windows Messenger with Voice and Video

Now that you have your Passport accounts set up, you can use the great new voice and video features of Windows Messenger. If both you and the person you want to have a conversation with have speakers, a microphone, and a video camera attached to your computer, having voice and video conversations is just as easy as having text conversations.

In this exercise, you are in your home office, which is located in a remote part of your house. Your Windows XP computer is connected to your home network and includes speakers, a microphone, and a video camera. Your spouse is in the kitchen using a Windows XP computer that is also connected to the network and has speakers, a microphone, and a video camera. Suppose that it's time to rally the troops for dinner (that means you!). Using Windows Messenger, not only can you have a voice conversation with your spouse, but you can see what's going on in the kitchen from the office and vice versa. First, you will tune your camera and your microphone to make sure they are set up properly for Windows Messaging. Then you will start Windows Messenger on each computer and initiate a voice or video conversation. Complete the following steps:

1 Make sure that both computers are connected to the Internet and that the microphone and camera are plugged in and installed.

2 On your Windows XP computer, in the Windows Messenger Window, on the Tools menu, click Audio And Video Tuning Wizard.

The Audio And Video Tuning Wizard appears, as shown on the next page.

3   Click Next.

The Select The Camera You Want To Use page appears.

4   Click the down arrow to the right of the Camera list, click the camera that you want to use for Windows Messaging in the drop-down list, and then click Next.

The next page of the wizard appears, instructing you to adjust your camera:

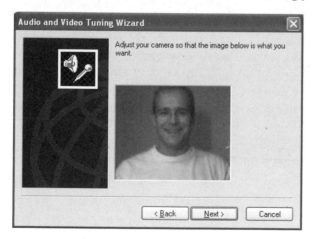

5   You will see a picture of yourself on the screen. Position the camera so that you appear in the picture as you would like to be seen. Click Next.

The next page of the wizard appears, giving tips on how to arrange your speakers and microphone.

6   Arrange your speakers and microphone, and then click Next.

The next page of the wizard appears.

7   In the Speakers list, click the name of the speakers you want to use for Windows Messaging, in the Microphone list, click the name of the microphone you want to use, and then click Next.

The next page of the wizard appears, instructing you to test your speakers.

8   Click the Click To Test Speakers button. Adjust the volume of your speakers to a level that you are comfortable with, and then click Stop. Click Next.

The next page of the wizard appears, instructing you to test your microphone.

9   Speak into the microphone, adjusting the volume until the meter is yellow. Click Next.

The Now Completed page appears.

10   Click Finish.

Send

11   On your computer, click the Send icon in the Windows Messenger window, and click your spouse's name in the drop-down list.

The Conversation window appears. The name in the title bar indicates the person you are communicating with.

12   Click Start Camera.

The camera screen appears. A notification pop-up window requesting a video and voice conference will appear on your spouse's computer.

13   On your spouse's computer, in the notification pop-up window, click Accept on the taskbar to accept the video conference.

Troubleshooting

If the Audio And Video Tuning Wizard appears on your spouse's computer, complete it just as you did on your own computer.

Both computers now have Video windows open.

You and your spouse can converse by speaking and can see each other on your video screens:

 Your computer

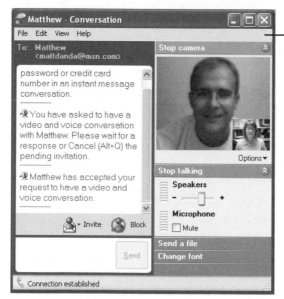 Your spouse's computer

Sending E-mail Messages

If the person that you want to send an instant message to isn't online when you want to send the message, you can send an e-mail message that can be read at the person's leisure. Whereas Windows Messenger sends and receives messages instantly, an e-mail account collects messages for you to look at later. Unlike instant messages, which are gone when you close the instant message window, e-mail messages are stored until you delete them.

E-mail accounts fall into two categories: Web-based and not Web-based. MSN Hotmail provides Web-based e-mail access, meaning that all e-mail messages are stored and managed through a Web site (*www.hotmail.com*). (When you sign up for a Passport, you receive a free MSN Hotmail e-mail account.)

To gain access to a Web-based e-mail account, you log on to the Web site using any Web browser on any computer with an Internet connection.

You may have an e-mail account that is not Web-based; for example, you might have an e-mail account with your Internet service provider (ISP). In that case, you can use Microsoft Outlook Express to connect to it:

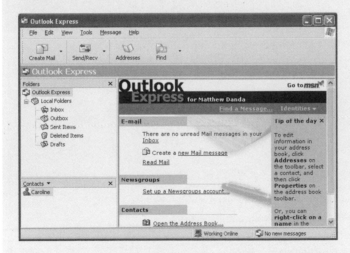

The primary difference between Web-based e-mail access and Outlook Express is that Outlook Express stores your messages on your computer, whereas a Web-based account keeps your messages on the Web server. With Outlook Express, you don't need to be connected to the Internet to review old messages or draft new ones, but with a Web-based account, you do. The disadvantage of using Outlook Express is that you will usually need to use the same computer to send and receive e-mail messages, whereas a Web-based e-mail account can be accessed from anywhere.

Using Windows Messenger to Transfer a File

With Windows Messenger, you can do more than have instant text, voice, and video conversations—you can also transfer files. You can use this feature while you're online to instantly exchange music, pictures, or any other files with others. Sending files through Windows Messenger gets the file to the receiver immediately, as opposed to e-mail, which could take some time.

In this exercise, you and your spouse are working on separate Windows XP computers in different rooms in your house. You'll now create a new Notepad document and use Windows Messenger to send a copy of the file to your spouse. Complete the following steps:

1   On your Windows XP computer, on the Start menu, point to All Programs, point to Accessories, and then click Notepad.

The Notepad window appears:

2   Type *This is an example file.*

3 On the File menu, click Save As.

The Save As dialog box appears.

4 In the File Name box, type *Test File*, and then click Save.

The file is saved in your My Documents folder.

Close

5 Click the Close button to close the Test File—Notepad window.

Notepad closes.

6 If the Windows Messenger window is not already visible, click the Windows Messenger icon on the taskbar, and then click Open on the pop-up menu. On the File menu, point to Send A File To, and then click your spouse's name in the list.

The Send A File To dialog box appears:

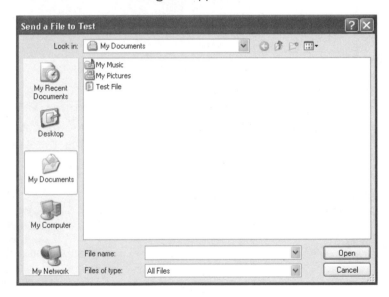

Tip

You can also open the Send A File To dialog box by clicking Send A File on the right side of the Windows Messenger window.

7 Click the My Documents icon on the left side of the Send A File To dialog box, and then double-click Test File in the list.

Your Conversation window indicates that you must wait for a response from your spouse:

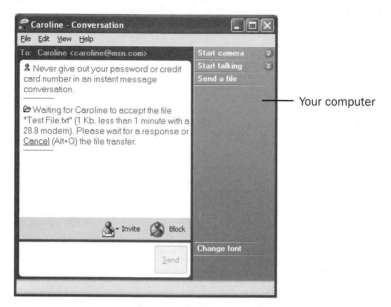

Your computer

Your spouse's Conversation window indicates that you would like to send a file, and your spouse must either accept or decline the invitation:

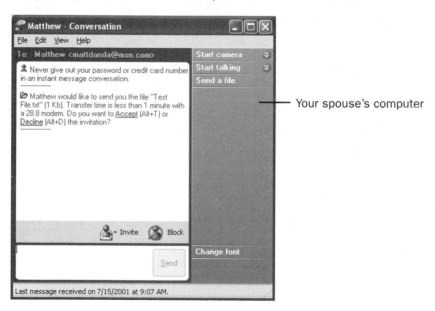

Your spouse's computer

8 On your spouse's computer, in the Conversation window, click Accept.

If a warning appears, indicating that files could contain viruses and that you should make sure that you trust the source, click OK.

On your computer, messages appear in the Conversation window, informing you that the invitation to transfer has been accepted, that the transfer has begun, and that it was successful.

Tip

When you first receive a file with Windows Messenger, Messenger creates a new folder in your My Documents folder called My Received Files. When you download files from other people, by default the files will be stored in the My Received Files folder.

On your spouse's computer, a message appears in the Conversation window, stating that the file was transferred successfully. Then a link appears, allowing your spouse to immediately open the file:

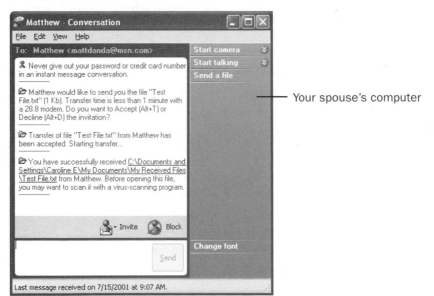

Your spouse's computer

9   On your spouse's computer, click the link to the Notepad file in the Conversation window.

The Notepad file opens.

10   Close the Notepad window by clicking its Close button.

Using Windows Messenger to Share Applications

Have you ever collaborated with someone on a project in which you had two computers but only one copy of a particular program to work with? Or have you tried to
explain what was happening with a program to a person seated at a computer some-
where else? With the Application Sharing feature in Windows Messenger, you can
share applications over the network so that you and a friend or associate can work
collaboratively on projects even if you are in different locations.

In this exercise, you and your spouse are working on separate Windows XP computers in different rooms in your house. You're playing the game Minesweeper, and you
would like some advice from your spouse. Rather than try to explain the situation,
you decide to use the Application Sharing feature of Windows Messenger to allow
your spouse to see the program and to temporarily control the program. Complete
the following steps:

1   On your Windows XP computer, on the Start menu, point to All Programs,
point to Games, and then click Minesweeper.

The Minesweeper window appears.

2   If the Windows Messenger window is not already visible, on the Windows
taskbar, click the Windows Messenger icon, and then click Open on the drop-
down menu.

3   In the Windows Messenger window, double-click your spouse's name in the
Online list.

The Conversation window opens.

4   In the Conversation window, on the File menu, point to Invite, and then click
To Start Application Sharing.

A message appears, indicating that you are inviting another person to participate in application sharing.

Tip

You can also click the Invite button and then click To Start Application Sharing.

5 On your spouse's computer, click Accept to accept the invitation.

On your computer, the Sharing Session and Sharing windows appear:

6 On your computer, in the Sharing window, click Minesweeper in the list of programs, and then click Share.

A check mark appears next to Minesweeper in the Sharing window, indicating that the application has been shared.

7 On your computer, click Minesweeper on the Windows taskbar.

On your spouse's computer, a window containing the Minesweeper program appears as shown on the following page.

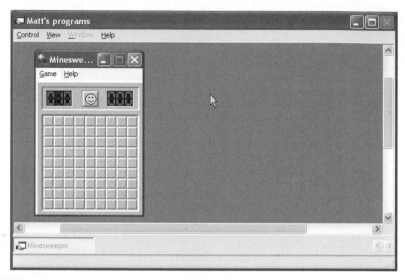

8   On your computer, click any square in the Minesweeper window.

    On your spouse's computer, an exact copy of the Minesweeper window is displayed.

9   On your computer, click the Sharing window on the Windows taskbar to activate it, and then click Allow Control.

    The Minesweeper program is now available for your spouse to control remotely.

10 Click Minesweeper on the Windows taskbar to activate it.

11 On your spouse's computer, on the Control menu, click Request Control.

    On your computer, the Request Control dialog box appears:

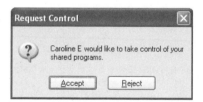

12 On your computer, click Accept.

    Your spouse now has temporary control of the Minesweeper program.

Tip

If you want to regain control at any time after you have given control of an application to a contact, simply press the Esc key.

13 In the shared Minesweeper program on your spouse's computer, on the Game menu, click New.

A new Minesweeper game appears in the Minesweeper windows on both your and your spouse's computers.

14 On your spouse's computer, on the Control menu, click Release Control.

Your spouse no longer has control of the Minesweeper program.

Close

15 On your computer, click the Close button to close the Minesweeper window.

The Minesweeper application closes and is no longer shared between the two computers.

Using the Whiteboard

Another useful feature of Windows Messenger is the Whiteboard. Whiteboard is a program that is very similar to Microsoft Paint (which allows you to draw pictures on your computer). However, with Whiteboard, every participant in your Windows Messenger conversation can see what you're drawing and can edit and modify your picture as well. Whiteboard can come in handy if you are collaborating on something that would be easier to understand with a graphic—for example, a blueprint or map.

To start Whiteboard, click the Invite button in a Conversation window, and then click To Start Whiteboard on the menu. You can also click Whiteboard in the Sharing Session window if it is open. You can then use the Whiteboard tools to create a graphic, or you can watch while the other people who are participating in the conversation do the drawing, as shown here:

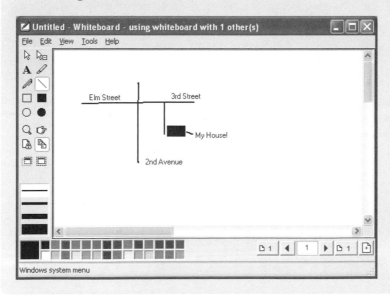

16   On your computer, click the Close button to close the Sharing window.

The Sharing window closes.

17   On your computer, click Close to close the Sharing Session window.

The sharing session is disconnected on both computers, but the Conversation window remains open.

Using Remote Assistance to Help Another Person

The Remote Assistance feature built into Windows Messenger makes it easy to help others who are having problems with their computers, or to ask for a contact to help you. If you've ever had to talk someone through fixing a computer problem over the phone, you will really appreciate this feature. You can even restart someone else's computer!

In this exercise, you and your spouse are working on separate Windows XP computers in different rooms in your house. Your spouse would like to change the amount of time that elapses before the screen saver appears, but he or she can't remember how. You are both signed in to Windows Messenger. You will now take control of your spouse's computer by using Windows Messenger's Remote Assistance feature, and you will then change the screen saver setting. Assuming that you have already opened the Windows Messenger window and initiated a conversation with your spouse, complete the following steps:

1   In the Conversation window on your spouse's computer, on the File menu, point to Invite, and then click To Start Remote Assistance.

On your computer, a message appears in the Conversation window indicating that you are being invited to start using Remote Assistance.

Tip

You can also start Remote Assistance by clicking the Invite button and then clicking To Start Remote Assistance.

2   On your computer, click Accept to accept the invitation.

The Remote Assistance window appears on your computer. It is currently blank because your spouse has not accepted the invitation yet.

On your spouse's computer, the Remote Assistance dialog box appears.

3   On your spouse's computer, in the Remote Assistance dialog box, click Yes to verify that you have permission to connect to the computer.

On your computer, the connection is established, and you are able to see your spouse's desktop in the right pane of the Remote Assistance window:

4 On your computer, click the Take Control button in the Remote Assistance window.

On your spouse's computer, the Remote Assistance—Web Page Dialog dialog box appears, asking if you would like to share control of this computer:

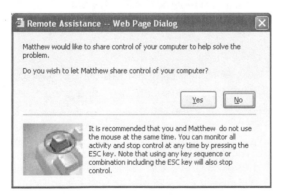

5 On your spouse's computer, click Yes in the Remote Assistance—Web Page Dialog dialog box.

On your computer, the Remote Assistance—Web Page Dialog dialog box appears:

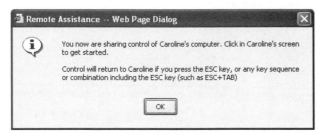

6 On your computer, click OK in the Remote Assistance—Web Page Dialog dialog box.

You can now control your spouse's computer using the Remote Assistance window.

Important

Your spouse can regain control of the computer at any time by pressing the Esc key or moving the mouse.

7 In the Remote Assistance window, right-click an empty area of your spouse's desktop, and click Properties on the shortcut menu.

The Display Properties dialog box appears.

8 In the Display Properties dialog box, click the Screen Saver tab, double-click in the Wait box, type *15*, and then click OK.

Tip

While someone else uses Remote Assistance to control your computer, avoid touching your mouse. If you move the mouse, you will take control of your computer away from the person who is assisting you.

9 On your computer, click the Release Control button in the Remote Assistance window.

You no longer have control of your spouse's computer.

Close

10 On your computer, click the Close button to close the Remote Assistance window.

11 On your spouse's computer, click OK in the Remote Assistance—Web Page Dialog dialog box, and click the Close buttons of the Remote Assistance window, the Conversation window, and the Windows Messenger window.

12 If you see a message stating that although you have closed the Windows Messenger window, the program will continue to run on the taskbar so that you can receive instant messages, click OK.

13 On your computer, click the Close buttons of the Conversation window and the Windows Messenger window.

14 If you see a message stating that although you have closed the Windows Messenger window, the program will continue to run on the taskbar so that you can receive instant messages, click OK.

Tip

You can also use Microsoft Outlook or Outlook Express to start Remote Assistance. In the Windows XP Help and Support Center, type *Remote Assistance* in the Search box, and then click Remote Assistance in the Help And Information list.

Taking Advantage of MSN Explorer

Having access to the Internet from all the computers on your home network is great. Now you might want to use MSN Explorer to get the most out of your Internet experience. MSN Explorer is an all-in-one browser that gives you quick access to e-mail, instant messaging, Web browsing, and your calendar, stocks, and photos. You can install MSN Explorer on every Windows computer on your network.

On a Windows XP computer, the first time you run MSN Explorer, a simple wizard guides you through the setup process, and you are up and running in no time. Thereafter, you simply click MSN Explorer on the Start menu to display the MSN Explorer logon screen. This screen looks very similar to the Windows XP logon screen:

Keep in mind that you can have multiple users of MSN Explorer on one computer and that the logon process for MSN Explorer is separate from the logon process of the Windows XP computer.

In this exercise, you would like to set up MSN Explorer on a Windows XP computer. You will start MSN Explorer and go through the MSN Explorer wizard.

Important

To complete this exercise, you need a dial-up ISP or broadband Internet access and a MSN Hotmail e-mail account.

Complete the following steps:

1   On the Start menu, click MSN Explorer.

The Welcome To MSN Explorer screen appears.

2   Click Continue.

The Please Tell Us Your Location page appears.

3   Click the down arrow to the right of the Country/Region box, click your country or region in the drop-down list, and then click Continue.

The Do You Want MSN Internet Access? page appears.

4   Select the No, I Already Have Internet Access option, and then click Continue.

The Do You Have An MSN Internet Access Dial-Up Account? page appears.

5   Select the No option, and then click Continue.

The Connecting page appears. MSN Explorer connects to the Internet and gathers information. The Do You Have One Of The Following E-mail Addresses? page appears.

6   Select the I Have An @hotmail.com E-mail Address option, and then click Continue.

The Please Enter Your Account Information page appears.

7   Type in your MSN Hotmail e-mail account and password, and then click Continue.

MSN Explorer verifies that the Hotmail account is valid. The MSN Terms Of Use page appears.

8   Read the terms of use, click I Accept The Agreement, and then click Continue.

The MSN Welcome screen opens and greets you:

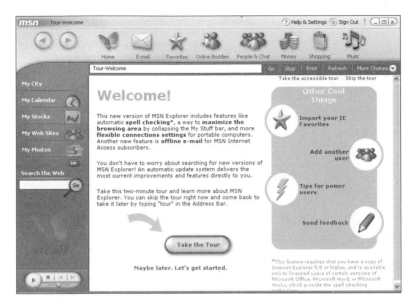

You can now read the instructions, take a tour, and start using MSN Explorer to streamline your Internet interactions.

Using MSN Explorer with Earlier Versions of Windows

Setting up MSN Explorer on a computer that is running an earlier version of Microsoft Windows is a bit more complex than setting it up on a Windows XP computer, because no MSN Explorer Wizard is available to help you.

In this exercise, you would like to use MSN Explorer on one of the Windows 98 Second Edition computers on your home network. To connect to the Internet and install MSN Explorer on your Windows 98 SE computer, complete the following steps:

1   On your Windows XP computer, connect to the Internet.

2   On the Windows 98 SE computer, start the Web browser.

3   In the Web browser's Address bar, type *http://explorer.msn.com/home.htm*, and then press Enter.

      The MSN Explorer home page appears.

4   In the list on the left side of the screen, click Install.

      The installation instructions appear.

5   Click the Install button that appears below the installation instructions.

The File Download dialog box appears:

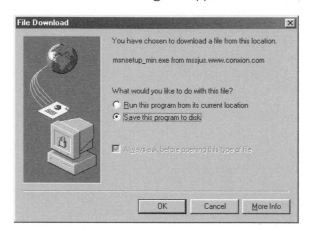

6   In the File Download dialog box, select the Run This Program From Its Current Location option, and then click OK.

The MSN Explorer setup program is downloaded, and the Security Warning dialog box appears.

7   In the Security Warning dialog box, click Yes.

The MSN Setup program starts:

8   Click Accept to accept the End User License Agreement.

The Welcome to MSN Explorer screen appears.

Tip

If you have a Web browser open, the Setup MSN dialog box prompts you to close it. Click OK to close your Web browser.

9   Click Continue.

The Do You Want MSN Internet Access? screen appears.

10   Select the No, I Already Have Internet Access option, and click Continue.

The Do You Have An MSN Internet Access Dial-Up Account? screen appears.

11   Click the No option, and then click Continue.

MSN Explorer connects to MSN and signs on, and then the Do You Have One Of The Following E-mail Addresses? screen appears.

12   Follow the instructions on the screen to enter your e-mail address or create a new one.

After you finish customizing MSN Explorer, MSN Explorer opens on your computer, and you can now take advantage of it to work efficiently on the Internet.

Chapter Wrap-Up

You have reached the end of this chapter and the end of the book. If you have finished using your computer for now, don't forget to log off.

Glossary

10/100baseT Cat5   A type of networking cable that supports frequencies up to 100 MHz and speeds up to 1000 Mbps.

backup   A copy of a file that is made to ensure that if the original file is damaged or destroyed, the loss will be minimized, and most if not all the data can be recovered. Typically, backups are made at regular intervals, stored on removable media such as Zip disks, and kept in a separate location from the computer.

broadband connection   A type of Internet connection that is relatively fast, always on, and suitable for exchanging large files such as graphics, video, or music over the Internet.

cable   A popular type of broadband connection that uses existing cable television wires to connect to the Internet. Cable connections are much faster than dial-up connections, require special cable modems, and do not interfere with television service.

Category 5 (Cat5) UTP   The industry standard for unshielded twisted-pair (UTP) cable that is used for connecting computers in a computer network.

coaxial   A type of cable that is composed of a copper wire surrounded by insulation and a grounded shield of wire mesh.

collaboration   *See* instant collaboration.

contacts   The people you communicate with on Windows Messenger. To be added to a Windows Messenger Contacts list, you must have a Passport account. In addition, you will need to have Windows Messenger installed and be connected to the Internet to communicate.

cookie   A small piece of data stored on your computer by a Web site. Cookies enable a Web site to recognize return visitors and allow it to store individual settings such as a logon name, password, and custom page settings.

default printer   The printer to which a computer sends documents if you select the Print command without first specifying which printer you want to use. You can have only one default printer at a time.

dial-up connection   A type of Internet connection that uses your telephone line to establish a connection. Dial-up connections are very popular but very slow. Your computer establishes an Internet connection using a modem over a telephone line and requires full use of your telephone line for the duration of the Internet session. Dial-up connections are suitable for occasional Internet use only, and are typically too slow for exchanging large files such as graphics, music, and video.

digital camera   A type of camera that stores pictures electronically as files, in a format that computers can read, manipulate, display, and exchange.

digital satellite system (DSS)   A type of dial-up connection that uses a satellite dish to download information from the Internet. Although a DSS dish can download information quickly, it is only one way, meaning that you must still establish a dial-up connection over a telephone line to begin the Internet session and upload information.

Digital Subscriber Line (DSL)   A popular type of broadband connection that takes advantage of unused bandwidth in regular telephone lines to exchange data. DSL is much faster than a dial-up connection or ISDN, but it doesn't interfere with regular phone use.

Ethernet crossover cable   A special type of Ethernet cable that allows two computers to connect directly to each other via their Ethernet network adapters. With normal Ethernet cable, each computer must connect to a network hub to communicate.

file server   A computer on a network that provides a central location to store files so that all other computers on the network can access them. Typically, a computer that acts as a file server has a large hard disk to store the files and some sort of backup device, such as a tape drive, to ensure that the files aren't lost or destroyed.

file transfer protocol (FTP)   An Internet service designed specifically for transferring files from one computer on the Internet to another. An FTP server on the Internet may contain large numbers of files, such as programs or images, that users on the Internet can download to their computers whenever they want.

firewall   A program or hardware device that helps prevent unauthorized access to a computer through a network connection. It monitors and filters packets that are sent and received, providing a barrier between a computer or a network and the outside world.

first-party cookie   A cookie placed on your computer by the Web site that you are visiting. *See also* third-party cookie.

flashcard reader   Some digital cameras have removable memory modules called *flashcards*. A flashcard reader is a device that you attach to your computer so that your computer can read the data stored on a flashcard.

gateway   A special computer, hardware device, or software program that resides between a computer or network and other networks. A gateway is typically used as a protective barrier between a network and the Internet, managing incoming and outgoing communications between the computers on the network and the Internet. *See also* hardware gateway.

guest   A type of user account that can access programs that have already been installed on the computer, but cannot change any system or user account settings. This account is ideal for someone who needs only temporary access to the computer—to surf the Web, for example.

guest computer   A computer that receives a connection from another computer, referred to as the *host computer*.

hardware gateway   A combination of hardware and software that connects a network to the Internet. A gateway typically also takes measures to make the computers on your home network safe from outside intruders. You can use a Windows XP computer as an Internet gateway for your network, or you can purchase a separate piece of hardware, also called a *gateway*, that you connect to your network and use to establish the Internet connection.

Home Phoneline Networking Alliance (HomePNA)   A group of industry experts who work to standardize the design of networks connected through home telephone lines. These standards encourage manufacturers to build devices that take advantage of home telephone wires, and they allow interoperability between different devices.

host   A computer that initiates a connection with another computer, referred to as the *guest computer*.

hub   *See* network hub.

Industry Standard Architecture (ISA) slot   A space in a computer where expansion cards, such as network adapters, can be installed. ISA slots are usually black, and they are generally found only in older computers.

Infrared (IR) port   A port on a computer, often with red plastic over it and a small light bulb underneath, that emits electromagnetic radiation, which allows for the transfer of data through the air.

instant collaboration   The ability to work with others in real time over the Internet. Collaboration includes transferring files, sharing a whiteboard for drawing, and collaboratively sharing and using applications such as Microsoft PowerPoint.

instant communications   An extension of instant messaging from text to other modes of communication, such as voice and video. A multimedia-capable PC, which includes speakers, microphone, or a headset, is required for voice; a Web camera is required for video.

instant messaging   A way of communicating on the Internet in which text messages are sent and received instantly. Unlike e-mail, which is stored on a mail server and can be downloaded and viewed by a recipient at any time, instant messages require that you be connected to the Internet and logged on to an instant messaging service or server.

Institute of Electrical and Electronics Engineers, Inc. (IEEE)   A technical professional organization that develops standards in electronics technology.

Integrated Services Digital Network (ISDN)   A type of dial-up connection that takes advantage of unused bandwidth over regular phone lines to exchange data. Transmission speeds for ISDN are faster than dial-up connections, but slower than DSL or cable. ISDN requires full use of your phone line to establish the connection and is typically more expensive than other options.

Internet connection   A connection to a worldwide network of computers. Your computer can connect using a modem and your phoneline, or through a broadband connection such as DSL or cable modem. When you are connected to the Internet, you have access to information stored on different computers all over the world.

Internet Connection Firewall   *See* firewall.

Internet Connection Sharing   A feature of Windows XP that allows multiple computers on a network to simultaneously use a single connection to the Internet.

Internet service provider (ISP)   A company or organization that maintains a direct connection to the Internet and allows you to gain access to it. Typically, you sign up with an ISP for a fee, and the ISP provides you with an access telephone number, user name, and password. Your computer uses this information to connect to a computer at the ISP, which in turn provides your computer with access to the Internet. In addition, most ISPs provide e-mail and customer support services.

Internet surfing   Using your Web browser to look at information stored on many different computers on the Internet. The information is accessed through *pages* that are organized as *Web sites*.

IP address   A special type of address that identifies a computer on a TCP/IP network. Because every computer on a TCP/IP network (such as the Internet) has an IP address, any computer can find and send messages to any other available computer on the network.

IPX/SPX   A type of communications protocol used by computers to communicate with each other on a network. IPX/SPX was invented by Novell and is typically used only on older networks or on networks that use Novell NetWare software. Most networks today favor TCP/IP over IPX/SPX because TCP/IP is the protocol used on the Internet.

log file   A file that records the actions performed by an application, service, or operating system.

mapping   Assigning a drive letter to a folder on the network so that it appears in the My Computer window.

Mbps (megabits per second)   A measure of bandwidth, or communication flow, over a network or other communications medium.

Microsoft Outlook Express   *See* Outlook Express.

Microsoft Windows Messenger   *See* Windows Messenger.

network adapter   A physical device that allows a computer to connect via a cable to other computers or devices to create a network. Sometimes called a *network interface*, a network adapter can be a card that you install in a computer or a USB device that you plug into a port in a computer.

network bridge   A piece of software or a hardware device that creates connections between different types of network media. For example, if you have an Ethernet network and a phoneline (HPNA) network, a network bridge makes it possible for the computers on those networks to communicate with each other. Windows XP includes a software network bridge that is easy to set up.

network card   A computer circuit board that is installed in a computer to allow it to connect to the network.

network hub   A type of hardware where cables come in from multiple computers and data is exchanged and sent out to the other computers on the network. It is an essential component of a typical Ethernet network.

network media   The collection of hardware such as hubs, cables, and network adapters that you use to physically connect computers and other devices to create a network.

Outlook Express   An e-mail program that comes free with Windows XP. Outlook Express makes it possible to quickly check your e-mail accounts. It also helps you keep track of the addresses and phone numbers of your friends and associates.

packet   A piece of information that can be easily routed through a network or the Internet. When a file is transmitted across a network, it is broken into small packets, and each packet is sent individually through the network. When all the packets reach the destination computer, they are reassembled by the destination computer to form a complete copy of the original file.

parallel   A type of communication that transmits data simultaneously over wires connected in parallel.

PC Card slot   An opening in the case of a computer, usually a laptop, designed to hold a PC Card, such as a network adapter.

Peripheral Components Interconnect (PCI) slot   A space in a computer where expansion cards, such as network adapters, can be installed. PCI slots are usually white.

peripherals   Hardware that is connected to a computer, such as printers, scanners, joysticks.

Platform for Privacy Preferences (P3P)   An emerging Internet standard designed to make it easy for Web sites to advertise their privacy policies and for users to specify their privacy preferences. For P3P to be effective, the Web site must specify its privacy policy using the P3P standard, and the user must use a P3P-compatible browser, such as Internet Explorer version 6.0.

Plug and Play   A feature that allows a computer to automatically detect and configure a device when it's plugged into the computer.

Plug and Play compatible   A device that, when plugged in, can be automatically recognized by Windows and enabled without interaction from a user.

port   A connection point on a computer that data can pass into and out of. Some ports are physical, such as the port that connects a printer to a computer, and some are virtual, such as the TCP/IP ports that a computer uses to communicate with other computers on the Internet.

printer driver   A program designed to allow other programs to work with a particular printer without concerning themselves with the specifics of the printer's hardware and internal language. By using printer drivers that handle the subtleties of each printer, programs can communicate properly with a variety of printers.

privacy policy   A document posted on a Web site that describes what information the Web site collects about you and what the organization plans to do with the information.

RJ-11   The standard modular jack used for telephone connections. It can have up to six pins but usually uses only four.

RJ-45 connector   The standard modular jack used for Ethernet networks. It has eight pins, sometimes called *positions*.

scanner   A device used to copy paper, slides, transparencies, or other media into a digital format, which can then be stored and manipulated on a computer.

serial   A type of communication that transmits data sequentially, one bit at a time, over a single cable. It is generally slower than parallel communication.

share name   The name you assign to a shared printer that other users will see when they connect to the printer on the network. You can change the share name using the Sharing tab of the Properties dialog box for the printer.

Shared Documents folder A folder on Windows XP computers that allows documents to be shared with other users of the computer, as well as other computers on the network. A folder with this name is also created on other Windows operating systems by the Windows XP Network Setup Wizard.

shared folder A folder that is accessible to other computers on the network.

streaming A method of delivering content in which content located on a server is transmitted across a network in a continuous flow and then played by client software. For example, by streaming music, the player can begin playing the music immediately instead of waiting for the entire music file to be downloaded to the computer.

TCP/IP The communications protocol used by computers on the Internet to communicate with each other. Because all computers on the Internet use TCP/IP, they can all successfully communicate. TCP/IP is also the protocol of choice for home or office networks that use Windows XP.

third-party cookie A cookie placed on your computer by a Web site other than the Web site that you are visiting. For example, many Web pages use content from other sources, such as advertisers, and these third-party sources can place a cookie on your computer. Third-party cookies are able to bypass many of the privacy safeguards built into cookies, which makes them a higher privacy risk. *See also* first-party cookie.

Trojan horse A program that masquerades as a legitimate program or file and attempts to bypass security measures and otherwise tricks users into opening a virus or other malicious program on their computers.

Universal Plug and Play (UPnP) Forum A group of over 350 companies that are defining an architectural framework for connecting electronic devices and services. The UPnP Forum is creating standards to enable connectivity and communication between Windows and intelligent appliances in the home, office, and other locations.

unshielded twisted pair (UTP) The most common kind of copper telephone wiring used in cables for creating networks.

USB port A standard Plug and Play interface between a computer and add-on devices. A USB port makes it easy to add devices to your computer without having to add an adapter card or even turn off the computer. You can add devices such as printers, joysticks, mice, keyboards, and network adapters.

virus A small program that sneaks onto a computer, usually performs some devious tasks, and then replicates and spreads itself to other computers. The proliferation of networks and the Internet has given viruses a new and efficient method for spreading.

virus protection software   A program that monitors a computer for known viruses and takes measures to defend the computer from them.

Web storage   A folder on the Internet in which you can store files. Web storage is a good service to use when you want to share photos, music, or videos with family and friends.

Windows Messenger   A Windows service that allows instant communication between a select group of people over the Internet. Unlike Internet chat programs, Windows Messenger allows only those that you want as part of the conversation to be included.

Index

M

Macintosh computers
adding to home network, 58
DAVE, 59
file format compatibility with
Windows computers, 59
network based on, adding
Windows computers to, 59
PC MACLAN, 59
TCP/IP protocol, 58
transferring files between
Windows computers, 59
understanding Windows
networking, 59
Macs. *See* Macintosh computers
making. *See* creating
malicious programs. *See* viruses
**manually setting up Internet
connections, 34**
**Map Network Drive dialog
box, 107**
mapped network drives
disconnecting, 109
removing, 109
mapping network drives, 107
Media Library, 96
adding to, from other
computers, 96
Media Player, 94
**messages, sending, to Windows
Messenger contacts, 135**
Microsoft Internet Explorer. *See*
Internet Explorer
**Microsoft Internet Referral
Service, 27**
Microsoft Outlook Express, 141
Microsoft Windows 95. *See*
Windows 95
Microsoft Windows 98. *See*
Windows 98
Microsoft Windows 2000. *See*
Windows 2000
Microsoft Windows Media Player.
See Windows Media Player
Microsoft Windows Messenger.
See Windows Messenger
**Microsoft Windows Millennium
Edition (Me), 47**
Microsoft Windows XP. *See*
Windows XP
Minesweeper, sharing, 146

modems, 26
setting up, 31
monitoring house remotely. *See*
home automation
monitoring packets, 73
Move Items dialog box, 89
moving
files, 89
files, to Shared Documents
folder, 88
Internet accounts, 32
**MS-DOS programs, printing
from, 122**
MSN Explorer, 153
downloading, 155
logon screen, 153
setting up, 154
starting, 153
with earlier versions of
Windows, 155
multi-player network games, 4
**multiple computers, reasons for
having, 1**
multiple pictures, selecting, 98
music
copying, 95
keeping track of, 96
listening to, on Windows XP
computer, 95
listening to, over the network, 95
organizing, 96
sharing, 95
streaming, 15
**My Computer window, displaying
folders in, 107**
My Documents folder, 90
creating files in, 88
displaying, 89
My Network Places window, 99, 101
adding network places to, 102
FTP sites, adding to, 103
My Received Files folder, 145

N

naming
computers, 45
Internet connections, 31
network places, 57, 104
shared folders, 92
shared printers, 122
user accounts, 69
workgroups, 45

network adapters, 16. *See also*
network cards
for broadband connections, 16
external, 18
installing, 18
internal, 16
for laptops, 18
Plug and Play, 17
network bridges, 20, 60
configuring, 20
and laptop computers, 55
network cards, 16. *See also*
network adapters
for laptops, 18
purchasing correct one, 17
network components, 51
Network Connection Wizard, 32
network drives
disconnecting, 109
mapped, removing, 109
mapping, 107
network games, 4
network hubs, 14
networking
printers (*see* shared printers;
printers, sharing)
removable disk drives (*see*
removable disk drives,
sharing)
network media cables. *See* cables
Network Neighborhood, 90
displaying, 90
network password, entering, 50
network places
adding, 57, 102
naming, 57, 104
networks. *See also* home
networks
accessing, 50
adapters (*see* network adapters)
ad hoc, 10
bridging (*see* network bridges)
choosing type, 7
components, 51
Ethernet (*see* Ethernet networks)
phoneline (*see* phoneline
networks)
power line, 9
types of, 8
using multiple types of, 20
wireless (*see* wireless networks)
Network Setup Disks, creating, 46

About the Authors

Matthew Danda is a computer consultant with a passion for absorbing convoluted technical information and then communicating it in terms that people can understand. His areas of specialty include network administration, Internet security and privacy, and software requirements analysis. When he's not in front of the computer, Matthew is usually training for another marathon or hanging out with his wife, Caroline. He is also the author of *Protect Yourself Online* (Microsoft Press, 2001) and lives in Prairie Village, Kansas. You can reach Matthew at *mdanda@secnetgroup.com*.

For the past seven years **Heather Brown** has worked at Microsoft Corporation, explaining complex technology in simple terms. Her newest challenge is making home networking both interesting and attainable to her mother. From this challenge came the idea of writing a step-by-step book for all the "moms" (and other non-techies) who want to take this next step in their mastery of computers. Besides meeting the needs of many people with this book, Heather hopes to reduce the amount of time she spends on the phone helping her family and friends figure out why "my printer in the other room won't work." In her spare time Heather is restoring a classic Lincoln Continental and remodeling her house. When she isn't "under the hood" in the shop out back, you can reach Heather at *HeatherTBrown@hotmail.com*.

The manuscript for this book was prepared and submitted to Microsoft Press in electronic form. Text files were prepared using Microsoft Word 2000. Pages were composed by Online Training Solutions, Inc. (OTSI) using Adobe FrameMaker+SGML 6.0, with text in Garamond and display type in Franklin Gothic.

Editing, production, and graphic services for this book were provided by OTSI. The hard-working project team included:

Project Editor:	Gale Nelson
Editorial Team:	Jan Bednarczuk
	Joyce Cox
	Nancy Depper
	Lisa Van Every
	Nealy White
Graphics & Production:	R.J. Cadranell
	Liz Clark

Contact OTSI at:

- E-mail: *info@otsiweb.com*
- Web site: *www.otsiweb.com*

Get a **Free**
e-mail newsletter, updates,
special offers, links to related books,
and more when you
register on line!

Register your Microsoft Press® title on our Web site and you'll get a FREE subscription to our e-mail newsletter, *Microsoft Press Book Connections.* You'll find out about newly released and upcoming books and learning tools, online events, software downloads, special offers and coupons for Microsoft Press customers, and information about major Microsoft® product releases. You can also read useful additional information about all the titles we publish, such as detailed book descriptions, tables of contents and indexes, sample chapters, links to related books and book series, author biographies, and reviews by other customers.

Registration is easy. Just visit this Web page and fill in your information:

http://www.microsoft.com/mspress/register

Microsoft®

- -